The Offshore Investment Guide

The "how to" of Global Investment

Lance Spicer

Trident Press

Copyright © Lance Spicer 2004

This book is copyright. All rights reserved. Apart from any fair dealing for the purpose of private study, research, criticism or review as permitted under the Copyright Act, no part of this publication may be reproduced, stored in a retrieval system, or transmitted in any form or by any means – electronic, mechanical, photocopying, recording or otherwise without prior written permission of the publisher.

Published by Trident Press Pty Limited
PO Box 3068, Bangor NSW 2234 Australia
Email: admin@tridentpress.com.au
Web Site: www.tridentpress.com.au

ISBN 0 9578539 4 7

First Edition March 2004

Australian Produced and Manufactured

Disclaimer

The material in this book is of the nature of general comment only, and neither purports nor intends to give any accounting, legal, tax or investment advice. Readers should not act on the basis of any matter in this book without first considering, and if appropriate taking, professional advice with due regard to their own particular circumstances. The author and publisher expressly disclaim all and any liability to any person or organisation, whether a purchaser of this book or not, in respect of anything, and of the consequences of anything done or omitted to be done by any such person in reliance, whether whole or partial, upon the whole or any part of the contents of this book. In no way is it the intention of the author or the publisher to encourage readers to evade tax or any lawful responsibility that they may have. The author and the publisher will not accept any responsibility for any errors or omissions. **Always seek professional advice from a Licensed Investment Adviser or Solicitor prior to acting upon any information in this book.**

Introduction to Lance Spicer

Lance Spicer was born in Sydney NSW in 1960. He worked for 16 years as an accountant, financial executive and consultant to several major Australian and foreign corporations including Australian and foreign banks. In 1990, his expertise was called upon to assist in the investigation of missing assets as a result of the Qintex collapse. Before "semi-retiring" he was the financial controller of a major listed property and tourism group. In recent years, he has become a professional investor in addition to writing 25 books on various subjects such as investment, financial privacy, small business and the share market. Twelve of Lance's books have now attained "best seller" status with books having been sold in over 75 countries around the world. Lance is a regular feature writer in magazines such as *Australian Business and Money Making Opportunities, Exposure* and *Small Business & Home Based Income*. In addition, he has spoken at several international and local seminars on issues of taxation, investment and privacy. His books have been featured on ABC Television's LateLine program and discussed on radio in the USA and in Australia. Lance's biography has recently been included in the Millennium Edition of Who's Who in the World.

The Offshore Investment Guide

Table of Contents

Introduction	**1**
Offshore Investment...... Is it worth it?	**5**
The Six Reasons Why You Need Offshore Funds in Your Long-Term Portfolio	11
International Tax Planning and Legalities	**13**
General Issues in Relation to Australian Tax	25
Withholding Tax	25
Capital Gains Tax	26
Controlled Foreign Company Rules	26
Transferor Trust Rules	27
Foreign Investment Fund and Foreign Life Assurance Policy Rules	28
Foreign Investment Funds (FIF) Legislation	29
The Good News	30
Things that Just Won't Work Anymore	30
Money laundering may be out of control, but.......	31
So, You Are Getting Some Tax Advice........	34
What is "Avoidance"?	34
Are You Liable to Taxation in the first place?	37
Offshore Basics	**40**
Frequently Asked Questions in Relation To Offshore Investment	40
Offshore Investing Myths Exposed!	56
Offshore for Different Reasons and Different People	57
Changes to The Offshore World	**59**
The Financial Action Task Force	59
The OECD Report of Harmful Tax Competition	60

The Offshore Investment Guide

Bearer Shares...... Finished or "Immobilised"?   61
Banking Changes   63
"Know Your Client" Requirements   63
Suspicious Activity – Money Laundering   64
Legislation Changes   65
The Future – 2004 Going Forward   66

Privacy   67

Hiding Money Offshore?..... But, Why & Where?   68
So, Who Shouldn't You Tell?   69
Investigators Are A Tricky Bunch   70

Asset Protection and the Nasty World of Litigation   72

Methods to Protect Yourself #1 – Simple Plan   75
Case Studies to Prove The Value Of Asset Protection   75
The Reality of Asset Seizure   77
Methods to Protect Yourself #2 – Company Plan   78
Methods to Protect Yourself #3 –Home Equity Plan   79
An Offshore Asset Protection Solution   80
Bringing The Ultimate Asset Protection Plan Together   81
The Onshore Asset Protection Plan   82
The Offshore Asset Protection Plan   82
Transferring My Assets to The Asset Protection Scheme   86
"Foundations" - Do They Work As An Asset Protection Vehicle?   87

Banking Issues   89

Advantages of Offshore Accounts   90
Procedure to Open an Offshore Bank Account   91
Internet and Private Banking   91
The Advantages of Banking with the Swiss   92
Offshore Banking – An Australian Perspective   94
Offshore Banking – A British Perspective   96
Offshore Banking – An American Perspective   100

How Offshore Works & Understanding Your Needs   105

The Offshore Investment Guide

The Offshore Structures – How they Work	108
The offshore company	108
The offshore trust	112
Who are you? What is your Scenario?	114
Australian	114
American	119
British	122

Investing Offshore   125

The Insignificance of the Australian Market	126
Diversification into global markets offers many advantages	127
Ways to Invest Offshore	129
Investments to get you started	130
Investment Concepts You Should Understand Before You Begin Investing	131
A Word of Warning!	135
The Biggest Mistake People Make	136
The Offshore Investing Process	140
An Offshore Bank Account	141
A Maildrop Address	141
The Broker	146
Do you need a Company or Trust?	146

Offshore for Different Reasons   149

The Real Estate Investor	149
The Business Person	156
The Asset Protector	161
The Equity & Fund Investor	161

International Investment Contacts   162

Due Diligence for Offshore Investors   168

Due Diligence Resources	170

Conclusion & Putting the Pieces Together   172

The "How To" of Global Investment

Introduction

Many people in the media and government would have us believe that Offshore Investing is for the very rich or the very "criminal".

They would have us believe that the only people that "go offshore", do so for dubious reasons, such as high profile Australians who have recently been under scrutiny such as investor, Rene Rivkin, Qantas executive and former federal minister, Graham Richardson.

They would have us believe that Offshore Investing is unsafe and there is a likelihood of losing all your money.

They would have us believe that you only go "offshore" to cheat on your taxes.

All of these "beliefs" are generalisations, and all generalisations are false!

These "beliefs" are propagated by those who have an "agenda". This agenda may be due to a government directive to protect us from ourselves. This could be due to the fact that so many people get caught up in scams that have emanated from offshore. The agenda could also be to stop the flow of funds out of this country and keep us investing principally here. On this basis it is best to keep us ignorant of the 98.5% of the world economy (and the corresponding percentage of investing opportunities). The other government agenda could be due to the fact that billions of dollars flow out of this country every year to invest offshore and that a good part of this money may or may not pay tax here ever again. This is the biggie! The Australian Tax Office and the government of the day, in recent years have become very concerned about this issue as have governments all over the world. So, in response to this they have put an extreme amount of effort into stopping or curtailing our "Offshore Investing" activities. Despite this, the flow of funds offshore continues, less for the wrong reasons, and more for the right reasons.

The Offshore Investment Guide

Governments to a large extent have "thrown the baby out with the bath water". Why I say this is because, for years in this country we have lamented the fact that we have seen Australian ownership of businesses, real estate and other assets go to foreign ownership. Have we not? Examples such as Arnotts, Vegemite, Qantas, all our banks, BHP and many others are either 100% foreign owned or have major foreign ownership stakes. What do we call this?...Foreign Ownership, of course. What do THEY call it?.............
Offshore Investment!

So, what is so wrong with us having a little foreign ownership? Nothing of course. This is called "Offshore Investment".

I wrote a little earlier about right and wrong reasons for Offshore Investing. I'd like to expand on this.
Let's look at the wrong reasons, and this is the area our "agenda" people focus on.... Probably a little too much.
- Illegal Tax Evasion and Tax Avoidance. This is the primary reason many people went offshore many years ago and to a minor extent still do so today. This is not Tax Planning.........It is illegal.
- Illegal Transfer of Assets. This is sometimes done to deprive a creditor of their rightful claim to assets owned by the transferor. This could be a business decision to deprive unsecured creditors of their claim or it could be as a result of a marriage or personal partnership where assets are removed out of the reach of any claim. This is NOT Asset Protection.... It is illegal.

There are probably a couple of other minor wrong reasons, but they all generally relate in one way or another to the illegal situations above.

Now, to the right reasons, and as you will see there are more right reasons for investing offshore than there are wrong ones.
- Offshore Investment Opportunities. This in my opinion is the "number one" reason for investing offshore. If this was the only right reason, it would still outweigh the wrong ones. As I mentioned earlier, 98.5% of all investment opportunities lie offshore.
Just a month ago, I checked how many managed funds around the world were earning returns of over 35%pa over a one, two and three year period and came up with over 150! I then checked how many of these were in Australia and came up with 2. What's more they had restrictive conditions on them that made them a little hard for the "average investor" to get involved with.

The "How To" of Global Investment

Why? We are such a small country and opportunities are limited. Why don't the top funds in the world list or operate here? Simple, we are too small, too restrictive and there is too much red tape for too little return. They can get all the capital they need operating in Europe or North America for instance. In a nutshell, as an Australian, you can invest offshore and take advantage of a larger number of opportunities or you can invest "onshore" and be limited to lesser returns and fewer opportunities to make money.

- Asset Protection. There is a big difference between Asset Protection and Illegal Transfer of Assets. Asset protection is done before you have problems. In fact, when there are no problems on the horizon. Illegal Transfer of Assets is done when you already have problems or there are claims pending on your assets. This is often called "Fraudulent Conversion" and can be overruled by the courts. Asset Protection is a wise move and should be undertaken regardless of whether onshore of offshore.
- Tax Planning. This is a very delicate area. However, done correctly, and legally, can benefit the offshore investor, even if it's only time deferral of a tax bill or utilising the benefits of offshore investing allowed for in the tax legislation already. However, telling lies on your tax return is very unwise and extremely illegal and above all very stupid. Having said that, you should never, ever invest in anything for tax reasons, the investment must stand alone on its potential growth or return benefits and tax being a minor secondary consideration.
- Estate Planning. This is a major consideration in countries that have death duties or estate taxes. By putting your assets in a non-taxable entity offshore, the effects of these "parasitic" taxes can be reduced. Thankfully, Australia has eliminated these appalling taxes…… hopefully forever.
- Privacy. Or more specifically, Financial Privacy. There are two schools of thought when it comes to financial privacy. The first one is that *"you don't need it! Simple as that. What are you hiding anyway?"* They believe that those seeking privacy are up to no good. I suppose they could be right.

However, this is not the case in all cases though, or possibly in many. Who are they to declare whether you have the "right" to privacy or not? This is where the second school comes in. These people believe they have the right to financial privacy regardless of the reason. Now, you may think you need a "real" reason to want privacy but who are we to judge what a real reason is? For example, there are more people than you realise out there that are paranoid about governments and corporations selling our information and our lives being compromised by the misuse of this information. Did I say, "paranoid"? mmmm, maybe on that basis I'm a little paranoid too. Anyway, there are also other

The Offshore Investment Guide

reasons where privacy may be desired, such as nosey business partners, prying relatives or malicious partners. Whatever, the reason, justified or not, we all have a right to financial privacy if we want it...... don't we?

As you can see the advantages of Offshore, International or Global investing are quite compelling and should not be overlooked by investors looking to maximise returns.

Which now brings us as to why this book was written. It was as a result of the many questions and requests for clarification on certain areas involving offshore investment. The purpose was to explore the practical applications of offshore investing and exactly how to go about and discuss the benefits and the disadvantages of different scenarios.

While my book, The Invisible World does touch on practical applications and related issues, it is more concerned with individual jurisdiction issues and contacts and explaining the differences, advantages and disadvantages of each country and most importantly the methodology of the whole thing. The Invisible World will be referred to a reference point several times in this book as it was not my intention for this book to supercede The Invisible World, but to supplement it. I suppose you could call this book "The Invisible World – Part 2".

I will explore the remaining issues of practical applications as well as a few others that just couldn't fit in The Invisible World that is now approaching 300 pages. This book will be a valuable companion to The Invisible World but can also be read as a stand-alone book and reference to the world of Offshore Investment.

All the best,

Lance Spicer
March 2004

The "How To" of Global Investment

Offshore Investment – Is It Worth It?

For many years tax, or avoidance of it, has been the driving force behind the whole 'offshore' thing. These days things are changing. The great majority of investors considering offshore investment, tax is not directly an issue. They mostly reside in high-tax places such as the EU, the US, Canada, UK, Australia or Japan, and they pay their tax, and if they make 'offshore' investments, it is in pursuit of higher returns, and without any intention to evade taxes in their home countries. This certainly is the case now, more so than it was say 15 years ago when dodging tax was a sport. These days the stakes are just too high, what with the crackdown on money laundering capturing more than one tax evader who became careless.

Of course some investors are lucky; they live outside high-tax areas, either as permanent or temporary residents. These investors can often avoid having to pay taxes on their investments, whether on or offshore, but that is due to the investor's circumstances, not the location of the investment. In essence, what I'm saying, it's all about the investment, not the tax benefits, or where you reside …… just the investment.

So why would an "offshore" investment be superior to an onshore investment other for reasons I explained in the introduction?

> **The problem is that well-meaning regulations act as a straightjacket for investment managers. They create an environment that is suitable generally for conservative and mediocre investment**

The first answer is because it is less regulated, and the behaviour of the offshore investment provider, whether he be a banker, fund manager, trustee stock-broker or whatever, is freer than it could be in a more regulated environment. Any government regulator will immediately say, "oh, of course, if it's unregulated, then it is riskier". Well, they would say that, wouldn't they? Some of these regulators really believe, the only safe place to invest is under their control, and if every country has it's own biased, narrow minded regulators then it's obvious to me that the

The Offshore Investment Guide

only safe place to invest is where they are in control........ and that would be everywhere.....right? Or am I being a little sarcastic? Seriously, though, some countries have over regulation due to laws being put in place for the lowest common denominator, that being an idiot who has no idea about investment and can't be trusted with his or her own money. I believe this is the case in many OECD nations. Other countries are a little more liberal and will allow you to make mistakes if you so wish, and they do tend to offer greater upside opportunity and that's what we're looking for.

However, getting back to government regulation, or over-regulation. It covers the avoidance of fraud (to protect investors from their own ignorance or stupidity), the avoidance of money-laundering (which has nothing to do with bona fide investors) and has prudential aspects, such as trying to prevent investment managers from making risky investments that could lead to loss for investors.

> "Lowest Common Denominator" legislation is enacted to protect investors from themselves, and therefore greatly constrain your choice and opportunity for above average profit. This gives "Offshore" an advantage.

The problem is that well-meaning regulations act as a straightjacket for investment managers. They create an environment that is suitable generally for conservative and mediocre investment, but one that is devoid of opportunities for the expert, or even for the moderately well-informed investor. Most people thinking about offshore investments are probably well above average in terms of their ability to avoid fraud (or should be), to understand markets, and to select superior investments. These people are ill-served by "lowest common denominator" regulation, and have to look outside their domestic markets for good returns.

This is not to say that good returns and risk can be easily separated. It's obvious that junk bonds are riskier investments than triple A debt instruments, and hence have a higher return. In the 1990's, Russian debt was all the rage and yielding 100% a year, a very risky investment indeed but the banks which invested in them for five years knew that, and were not surprised when they lost their capital in 1998 when it all fell apart, even though they made a song and dance about it after the event.

In recent times "Hedge" funds have shown us the benefits of "investment freedom" very clearly. They almost all chose "offshore" bases, mostly for regulatory reasons, and their high minimum investment levels will have put off the vulnerable types of investor who

The "How To" of Global Investment

have little understanding of the risk involved. However, most investors in these funds have received returns of 20% or 30% a year for ten to fifteen years, before moderate recent losses. George Soros's decision to pull back from some types of hedge fund, in the investors' best interests, show that the market is the best regulator if it is given freedom. Hysterical accusations that hedge funds increase market volatility are far from the truth. If anything, the opposite is the case. It is the dramatic increase in global liquidity that has increased the apparent size of swings. Hedge funds and derivatives tend to dampen volatility, not increase it according to most economists and investment professionals.

It is also far from the truth to say that "onshore = safe" and "offshore = risky". Many offshore jurisdictions have high-quality regulatory regimes that quite clearly separate the overly risky investment from the well-managed and sensible investment, without constraining investor choice and opportunity. Unlike in some countries, as I've said before, "Lowest Common Denominator" legislation to protect investors from themselves, and therefore greatly constrain your choice and opportunity for above average profit.

Lower Tax

I'm often asked, "Why do certain investment managers set themselves up in Offshore Financial Centres or "tax havens"? Mainly due to the fact not only does the fund escape paying tax, but more importantly from the managers point of view, so do they. It means they can charge a "market" or "below market" rate for their management of the fund, but end up with a better overall profit due to the lack of taxes. All jurisdictions, whether they are tax low or high, give some tax advantages to certain preferred types of investment, usually starting with the government's own bonds, which are often tax-exempt (why else would anyone buy them?). In high-tax countries, most of these exemptions apply only for small or specific investments, and seldom to high-return investments.

What is a double taxation treaty?
An agreement between two countries intended to relieve persons who would otherwise be subject to tax in both countries from being taxed twice in respect of the same transactions or events. By and large, most offshore jurisdictions do not have double taxation treaties, since they don't have much local taxation. Offshore jurisdictions, which do have double tax treaties usually cannot use them to benefit investors receiving complete local tax exemption

The Offshore Investment Guide

Also, investment managers in low-tax areas have a considerable tax advantage over their colleagues in high-tax areas, which are eventually reflected in better returns for the investor. Offshore jurisdictions which, have good double-tax treaty networks (surprisingly, there are quite a few) are often able to receive investment income even from high-tax countries without the imposition of withholding tax, and usually offer tax-exempt or tax-reduced local laws, so that the final investor has access to gains in a fund or an investment with little or no intervening taxation. It's obvious that a fund which pays a composite rate of 10% tax on its profits will grow much more quickly that one which pays 30%, and differentials on this scale are easy to achieve just as a result of picking a low-tax base as against a high-tax base.

In addition, bank interest is rarely subject to withholding taxation in offshore jurisdictions, so that a money market fund is going to grow more quickly offshore than in a country, which imposes 30% corporation tax on its gains. Of course, if you are resident in a high-tax area, the taxman will ensure that you pay the higher rate on your gains, but it may be at a lower rate of Capital Gains Tax.

"Alternative" Offshore Investment

"Alternative Offshore Investment" is one of those terms, which is easier to define by saying what it is not, rather than by saying what it is. The investment opportunities on offer to the average, moderately well informed person living in an OECD country are limited by the regulatory structures of the country one lives in, by lack of knowledge on the part of financial intermediaries, and to some extent by fear of the unknown. Therefore, stock exchange investment starts becoming a lot more awkward, the further "Offshore" one tries to invest. Many types of offshore fund cannot even be marketed at all in most high-tax countries.

The investment options tend to narrow themselves to local stock markets, funds or investments, which conform to tight investment and regulatory guidelines and the investment products of financial institutions. Not very exciting and certainly not "the best of the best" you are looking for.
"Alternative Offshore Investment" can be defined as everything else.
Various events have tended to broaden the range of accessible offshore investment options over the last ten years, for instance:
- In Europe in particular, the growth of the EU single market has forcibly demolished exchange and capital controls, and has again increased the level of competition in financial products.
- The rapid growth of 'offshore', in response to ever-increasing levels of financial sophistication on the part of investors.

The "How To" of Global Investment

- Finally, and most importantly, the Internet has provided financial institutions with the ability to offer their products directly to retail customers, by-passing geographical restrictions, and making regulatory compliance optional for the end-user.

Alongside this increase in accessibility, there has been a parallel increase in diversity, particularly in investment or mutual funds. Twenty or thirty years ago, funds were little more than "safe" ways of investing in local stock markets without the hassle of going through an expensive stockbroker, who probably had no idea anyway. While such funds still exist and make up the majority of funds available, they are regarded as pretty much a waste of time by "alternative" investors seeking better returns from offshore funds involved in things such as property, currencies, emerging markets, derivatives, bonds, and of course equities. These days, think of some unusual investment and there will be a fund to invest in it.

However, There Is a Downside

Offshore investment is not necessarily riskier than onshore investment. People making offshore investments, that is direct with offshore providers rather than through onshore and therefore regulated sellers of offshore investments, must do so with their eyes open. In most cases, and for all but the most experienced investors, this means take advice. Even if you are eventually going to trust your own judgment, or make a deliberately risky investment with money you can afford to lose, there is everything to be said for taking advice from wherever you can get it, other than from the person selling you the investment of course.

It is probably obvious that getting information about offshore investments can be difficult. There is a wealth of information available about onshore investment or about regulated offshore funds marketed onshore, from the newspapers and from a multitude of other sources. It can be much harder to find out about offshore investments directly. It is also harder to track investments once you have made them, although some traditional difficulties have more or less disappeared: the telephones work nowadays, and almost all offshore jurisdictions have supervisory regimes, which exclude the bandits.

But offshore providers and advisers can still be astonishingly laid-back sometimes (remember, it is probably thirty degrees Celsius and going home time when you call).

Remember also that a tropical island with a population of 20,000 people and 40,000 international business companies may not leap to push your liability claim against one of its senior professionals through the courts,

The Offshore Investment Guide

however good its investor protection laws may be. 'Caveat emptor' ('Buyer Beware' – for those of you who missed high school Latin) is not a phrase that is well understood in OECD countries any longer, but it still has resonance offshore.

So, Is It Worth It?

After having read all that, your answer is probably "Yes, it is worth it", or hope that's your answer, but I'm a realistic enough to know that your real answer probably, "Yes, it's worth looking into.... Then I'll decide". The other thing that's probably crossed your mind is that all that I've written needs to be backed up with proof of offshore investments providing better returns than domestic ones. So, here is some proof:

- JF Asia Absolute Return Fund – Averaged 144%pa last 5 years
- Gresham House – Averaged 185%pa last 4 years
- AHL Currency Fund – Averaged 45% last 3 years

These returns quoted as at 30September 2003

Now, I challenge you to find one, just one Australian fund that has performed as well as any of these over the last 3-5 years! I've looked in the Australian Financial Review and it's littered with mediocre, safe, "keep up with the market" funds returning somewhere between negative returns and percentage returns in the low 20s at best. Is this good enough? Mind you the ones that made into the 20s were very rare. What is your Super Fund or Managed Fund investment doing? Are you happy with the returns? This is what happens in a strictly regulated environment. While I don't disagree with some of our laws and agree they need to be there, the restrictions and penalties are so onerous, that many managers just play it safe at the expense of great returns. Except for a couple of aggressive and unconventional fund managers, Australia is a bit of a 'mediocre investment wasteland'.

You think 'mediocre investment wasteland' sounds a bit harsh.... doesn't it? Well, to a certain extent it's true, but we can't just blame timid money management brought about by over regulation and over government. There is a factor of size that we spoke about earlier. The size I refer to is 1.5%..... Australia's economy, bringing with it limited opportunity. Keep thinking about the 98.5% outside of Australia.

The "How To" of Global Investment

The Six Reasons Why You Need Offshore Funds in Your Long-Term Portfolio

1. **Greater choice.** The overwhelming majority of mutual funds traded worldwide aren't available to Australians. Indeed, of the more than 80,000 funds trading worldwide, only a handful, are available here.

2. **Offshore funds can take speculative positions prohibited by domestic securities laws.** It's very difficult for a fund traded on Australian and US markets to switch from a long (bullish) to short (bearish) position without expensive and time-consuming approval from regulators. Yet in the hands of an experienced portfolio manager, this kind of flexibility can lead to exceptional long-term profits.

3. **Offshore funds can employ risk-hedging techniques.** This strategy can actually make offshore funds safer than domestic funds. For instance, Australian managed funds can't shift their focus to the futures markets without obtaining clearance from the ASIC particularly if it is outside the terms of their prospectus, even if these markets look far more promising to the fund managers. Such restrictions are virtually non-existent in properly chosen offshore jurisdictions.

4. **Offshore funds can offer foreign currency diversification.** Many offshore funds are denominated in the euro, Swiss franc or British pound, unlike local funds being in Australian dollars.

5. **Offshore funds offer privacy.** Offshore funds take your wealth off the domestic "radar screen" and make it invisible to predatory lawyers and the myriad asset tracking services that can determine the owner.

6. **Offshore funds can be held in retirement or superannuation plans.** There are no restrictions on placing offshore funds in retirement plans, although you must find a trustee or manager willing to administer your plan if it contains foreign assets. Ideal for a Self-Managed Super Plan though.

If you would like the facts and figures on some of the best performing investments in the world, I suggest you read my two High Yield Investment books. Between them they have listed around 130 of the world's best performing investments. These books do not contain my opinions, nor my advice on what to invest in. They simply list

The Offshore Investment Guide

investments, give you a rundown of what they are, how they work, their returns and how to contact and invest with them. They have been compiled by researching companies like Standard and Poors, Moody's, Morningstar, Fund Managers themselves and the consensus of brokers around the world. There is a catalogue at the back of this book to order.

"The freedom and happiness of man are the sole objects of legitimate government. Oppose with manly firmness and invasions on the rights of the people"
– Thomas Jefferson, US President

The "How To" of Global Investment
International Tax Planning and Legalities

There have been some enormous changes in recent years. The "offshore world" is now coming to terms with another wave of changes, brought about by the desire of western governments to crack down on tax minimisation....... Oops, sorry I meant money laundering. I apologise for the cynicism, but it sometimes seems that their efforts are more directed at aggressive tax planning than genuine money laundering. Whichever way you look at it, recent changes have made us re-think how we approach things with tax and legalities and have made us a little more conservative in our views. Am I softening my stance on aggressive tax planning? A little I suppose, but the world is changing and becoming a lot less liberal and a lot more restrictive and regulated.

So, we must adapt to the new regime, and make money the best way we can while still staying well within the bounds of the law. There are still things we can do. In fact, Australian Tax Laws have changed little under this new regime. However, we have to be mindful that while we may not be breaking the law, our activities could be regarded as suspicious under the new guidelines and that could bring with it a whole lot of attention you just don't need in your life. I'm talking about a "Bureaucratic Financial Enema" or "BFE"!

Tax planning or is it sometimes called in the offshore world, "tax mitigation" has up until recently been used by investors employing a variety of different approaches. For instance:

Legal Tax Minimisation. In essence, there were three distinct and separate approaches, derived entirely from different legal traditions.

- The British approach, which meant finding "loop-holes" in the legislation, by interpreting words in ways that had been overlooked by Parliament or creating situations that had not been foreseen by Parliament. This is the one employed by many Australian accountants and tax planners.

The Offshore Investment Guide

- The US approach, which assumed that there were no "loopholes". In the US, tax planning is about identifying and using mechanisms known and approved by the legislation. For example, the legislation greatly encourages Americans to provide for their old age, and in charitable giving.

- The continental European approach, where the concept of "abuse of the law" makes the British approach impossible. Here, the Civil Law is much harsher than British Common Law. The result, of course, was that tax avoidance, as we understand it, did not exist. Hence the complete confusion in the minds of French bureaucrats as to the difference between tax evasion and tax avoidance.

Unlawful Tax Evasion. This relied entirely on concealment and secrecy for its effectiveness. There were, in this area too, distinct traditions.

- The Swiss approach. This relied on the policy of a complete blanket of secrecy on all information. It led to "numbered" accounts, where knowledge of the identity of the owner was rigorously protected and restricted. (It also led to vast amounts of unclaimed deposits over the years, as owners of numbered accounts died without any relatives knowing of the accounts.)

- The Caribbean/British tradition. This system relies on the use of 'fronting' companies and trusts, in particular, using companies where there was minimal information available publicly. It relied on the international community recognising the legitimacy of such companies, notwithstanding the lack of information available on them, their owners, or managers. It even led, in some jurisdictions, to "secrecy" legislation making it a criminal offence to give information not lawfully public (trying to emulate the Swiss approach).

- The cash or Russian approach. This is the oldest system of all, in which transactions took place on a barter or cash basis, where the medium of exchange never sees any bank and is never recorded. Settlement of obligations takes place in a foreign currency outside the country. This is very much the system in use in Russia today, where US dollar bills are the "settlement" currency.

In recent years, there has been a spectacular increase in both lawful tax minimisation and in unlawful tax evasion. As a result it was absolutely

The "How To" of Global Investment

inevitable that it would attract the attention of the OECD and the member countries including Australia, the US and the UK), who began to feel threatened. There has always been a total predictability that this was going to happen. Simply put, it was costing them too much money in lost revenue and they needed to restrict the flow in some way, and the money- laundering thing did in fact "kill two birds with one stone".

This attack, over recent years, by the OECD and their member nations, can be described as a three-pronged attack as explained below:

The First Prong - Ever-tightening tax systems.

- The tax systems of the world have become far more sophisticated, co-ordinated and effective. The British "loop-hole" system is declining, as attitudes change and the Courts alter their attitudes too. The Inland Revenue is far more likely to assume that a so-called "Tax Avoidance" programme is, in fact merely a facade behind which hides a fraudulent tax evasion scam.

- In the USA, the penalties for using foreign corporations have made such use counter-productive. The changes in the tax rules on trusts have made foreign trusts simply ineffective for US tax planning except in a handful of very limited situations. The simple use of an overseas company or trust to conceal taxable events is now downright dangerous. The use of secret bank accounts has also become downright dangerous.

- The number of "black lists" is ever increasing. Transactions with countries on such black lists are subject to special scrutiny.

The Second Prong - Attack Secrecy.

This has been aimed at producing transparency and the free exchange of information. The arguments relating to "Harmful Tax Competition" are, as we all know, in reality a huge smokescreen. What lies behind these erroneous and ill-thought out arguments is, real enough. It is the desire to implement a world-wide convention whereby tax authorities freely exchange information amongst each other, and, in addition, will seek out information when requested to do so. It represents a complete reversal of the former traditional principle that the tax affairs of one country are uniquely theirs, and not a matter for any other country to be concerned in.

The Offshore Investment Guide

The Third and Final Prong - Imposition of Regulation.

This has been done in the name of defeating criminal money laundering. This too has been inevitable. As globalisation of business and culture followed the explosion in communications, so too did crime. The war against crime was bound to follow.

As a result, the full weight of the international establishment is directed against the use of financial institutions for the concealment of crime, fraud and tax evasion.

> **Is Tax Planning dead due to all the new laws and attacks on secrecy? Is it a dying industry?**
> **Far from it!**

So, where does this leave tax planning? Is it a dying industry? Far from it! The international tax planning industry remains alive and well. However, the rules have changed, and the culture has changed, and practitioners must change their practices too, or go out of business.

I can say, with certainty that the days of unlawful tax evasion are drawing to a close. Tax evasion is now very definitely a criminal matter, and fraudulent tax evaders are criminals. The Banker who aids and helps a criminal to operate a bank account is an accessory to a crime, and that is the same whether the customer is an Australian tax evader, a Dutch drug pusher, or an Italian Mafia member.

> **Legal requirements not only in the country of establishment must be observed, but also in the resident country of the directors, shareholders, trustees and beneficiaries.**

The "Know-Your-Customer" rules are making the use of the traditional "anonymous" companies and trusts almost impossible, especially where, such information can be accessed by the fiscal authorities on request.

Careful, planning is now required when using offshore entities. Legal requirements not only in the country of establishment must be observed, but also in the country of the directors, shareholders, trustees and beneficiaries.

The "How To" of Global Investment

The rules relating to the handling of cash are making the use of cash extremely difficult, and this isolates the cash-using criminal fraternity. However, as the old declines, the new growth takes its place. So what are these new techniques?

Tax planning should work "with" the legislation, and not "against" it. Planners must identify what is lawful, and follow these avenues.

The use of Offshore Companies and Trusts is not finished, but there does need to be a re-evaluation as to why people would need them. To avoid tax in itself is no longer a good enough reason. You should establish a structure offshore only because you need one to undertake asset protection, access investments that you are unable to otherwise invest in without an offshore entity or for any other reason than criminal activity.......... And tax evasion is a criminal activity.

Let's now look at five examples of how people have used offshore structures and then examine if they have done the right thing or left themselves open to trouble down the track.

> ## ATO – Tax Haven dealings legitimate
> *"Many dealings with tax havens are legitimate. Tax havens can provide genuine finance, insurance, broking, holding company and head office services..... Tax havens are particularly attractive to international business involved in portfolio management, such as insurance, hedge and mutual funds and offshore investment funds. Because of this, we see large monetary flows between Australia and tax havens in relation to currency trading"*
> – Australian Taxation Office, February 2004

- **Example 1 – Cleaning Business**

The Story

Mark has worked for the same company for 20 years. He has reached the top of the ladder in his department but the pay is good and he can't afford to quit. He's getting tired of paying taxes and would like to earn extra money. Last year he and his wife Mary started a home-based business doing cleaning work for small to medium size companies in the city where they live. Most of the money they receive is either cash or

The Offshore Investment Guide

cheques. Mark was surfing the Internet a few months ago and found an ad for offshore services offering to set up a company, including a bank debit card and cheque cashing service for "under $1,000". The offshore advisor suggested that they could set up an offshore corporation (Clean-It Ltd.), which would own their business. They could then deposit cheques made payable to Clean-It Inc. and withdraw the money at home using a debit card, which leaves no paper trail at home.

He assured them that the account would be confidential, so they wouldn't have to worry about prying income tax inspectors. To add another level of security, the promoter suggested they set up an offshore trust which would own the shares of the cleaning business and be the ultimate home of the income. That way, Mark and Mary don't own anything, because, the funds are controlled by an offshore trustee, whom is sworn to secrecy, so no one will be the wiser. The promoter assured them that this way all the money Clean-It Inc. earned would be tax-free.

The Reality

It's easy to see that Mark and Mary have opened themselves up to a whole heap of trouble. Assuming they live in Australia, the law imposes stiff penalties for tax evasion and that is what they are doing. They are sending taxable earnings to their offshore company without declaring it and then bringing it back via a debit card and spending it tax-free. If they don't tell anyone and are very careful about what they buy, they may get away with it, for a while.

The cheques they receive from their clients are usually under $1,000 and the clients may not know that the funds are going to an offshore company. If the cheques are over $1,000, the risk of being caught goes up because the banks must keep records of all such payments going out of the country for the tax officials.

If Mark and Mary or one of their clients are audited, the risk of detection is high, especially if clients are claiming the cleaning expenses for income tax purposes. Often tax departments will check expenses deducted from one taxpayers' income against income claimed by the recipient. Since Mark and Mary aren't declaring any of the income, it wouldn't take a Sherlock Holmes to catch them at their game.

If they buy real estate, cars, furniture or holidays using their debit card, they also greatly increase the risk of being caught. One of the major weapons used by the Australian Tax Office is unsupported life style change. They look at the taxpayers' income and expenditures. Again, it doesn't take a genius to see through a plot if expenditures exceed

The "How To" of Global Investment

declared income. Furthermore, the rules governing trusts in Australia have been substantially tightened in recent years.

The bottom line here is what they are doing is illegal and they may face stiff penalties. Jail is not out of the question. The ATO is cracking down on this type of thing can trace the funds being transferred by using the AUSTRAC system.

- **Example 2 – Equipment Hire Company**

The Story

Frank owns a company that leases cranes, forklifts and other heavy equipment to construction companies in a number of countries. With the help of an offshore advisor recommended by a friend, Frank 'sold' the leasing company to an offshore company, (we'll call it "ABC") that now buys the equipment and leases it to other companies around the world. Frank retains a small interest in the company and the rest is owned by an offshore trust and an International Business Company (IBC). Furthermore, ABC can sell the equipment after it has been leased a number of times and retain the capital to buy more equipment tax-free.

The Reality

This example is a little more complicated. If Frank legitimately leases heavy equipment to companies around the world and has corporations offshore for reasons other than tax avoidance at home, there are a number of potential benefits. The tax haven or havens he chooses will determine his tax bill at home. He could set up in a tax haven where his company pays no tax on earnings such as the Cayman Islands, or the Turks and Caicos Islands, but he might be better advised to also use an intermediary company in a country with tax treaties with the countries where he leases his equipment. Rather than lose 25-30% to withholding taxes in the high tax countries where he does business, this amount could be substantially reduced. It will cost him more to set up an intermediary company, but the strategy will reward him with the best of both worlds: complete privacy and liability protection as well as potential tax savings.

However, there is another consideration. If Frank's company is set up in a pure tax haven to which he travels and sends money, his chances of an audit are greatly increased, even if he has done nothing wrong. Revenue officials carefully scrutinise any movement to and from well-known, high profile tax havens. If they see that an individual has made a number of trips and sent money to such countries, a red flag goes up. If,

The Offshore Investment Guide

on the other hand, Frank has an intermediary company in, for example, the Netherlands, which has a number of favourable tax treaties, owned by another company in, for example, the Netherlands Antilles, he reduces this risk. Business trips and money sent to (and from) tax treaty countries don't usually elicit the same interest from tax officials.

The bottom line here is, if this arrangement has been established to avoid tax, Frank has a problem. Under the Anti-Avoidance legislation (Section 4a of the Act) it could be deemed a tax avoidance scheme and tax plus penalties could be imposed. There must be a commercial reason for Frank to do what he has done. He should also be aware of "Transfer Pricing" as a form of avoidance – This could be deemed illegal activity.

- **Example 3 – A Writer**

The Story

Another one that is a little tricky.... Peter is a writer who writes screenplays for well-known film companies and is well paid for his labours. His offshore consultant has helped him set up an offshore company that now collects his sizable fees. Peter is paid a smaller fee that he is taxed on at home. His offshore company purchased a villa in the French Riviera that Peter has exclusive use of, while in Europe on business.

The Reality
This story is commonplace and is often asked if it's ok to have a simple setup such as this. Peter, can benefit from setting up a company in a tax haven as long as he has legitimate reasons for doing so, and they are for other than simply tax avoidance. If he sells his work to a number of different companies in different countries, it could be argued that an international company in a tax haven gives him greater access to business worldwide with fewer restrictions, even if he continues to reside in a high tax country. He could sell the rights to his work to an offshore company for a fee and receive income that is declared at home. He could take the income as a royalty or dividend, which are given favourable tax treatment, depending on the countries involved. He, too, may find it beneficial to use an intermediary company in a tax treaty country as well as a tax haven to reduce taxes and give him protection from future creditors at home.

However, Peter must be careful to meet all Foreign Investment Fund (FIF, which includes companies and trusts) requirements necessary to reduce or defer taxes payable at home. For instance, he must have no

The "How To" of Global Investment

beneficial interest in the offshore company. Section 488 of the Australian Taxation Act makes it quite clear that your name does not have to be on a share certificate or share register of a foreign company as the legal owner of those shares to be deemed a beneficiary. You will be deemed to have an interest in a FIF if you have a beneficial interest in that FIF even without the legal title to it, if so decided by the ATO. The ATO determines this by having evidence that you have had dealings with the establishment of the company in the first place.

So, if he held shares in the company or was a director or even had control of the company in some way – he would be deemed to have an interest, obviously. If he was not a shareholder, nor director, nor had any bits of paper that stated he had an "interest" in the company, then he would be deemed to not have an interest under the law and the accrued income or gains of that company would be taxable in Australia.

However, there is good news, there is an exemption for an interest of $A50 000 or less. A small investor exemption is provided for both direct and indirect interests in FIFs. The exemption is only available if you are a natural person and your interest, together with those of your associates (any family members, business partners and related entities), in FIFs, and resident public unit trusts is $A50 000 or less at the end of the financial year. [SECTIONS 96A and 515 of the Income Assessment Act] This does not mean you don't have to pay tax, but only when it's repatriated and in your hands like normal income.

So, bottom line, if his interest in the offshore company at 30 June is AUD$50,000 or less, then he does not come under the FIF rules and can therefore take advantage of the exemption until income is in his hands. Peter can make his arrangements legally but must keep his interest in this company below the threshold and must at all times ensure that the purpose of the offshore entity is not tax avoidance and he has commercial reasons for the setup. I often wonder how the ATO can enforce all this stuff. They would need a staff of 500,000 to control this properly in my opinion.

- **Example 4 – Internet Business**

The Story

William is an American author who writes booklets, which he sells on the Internet. His market has grown and he now sells to clients in many countries. He realises that to market worldwide, he needs an international presence. The cost and quality of printing dictates that his books be printed in a relatively high tax country which also has very

21

The Offshore Investment Guide

strict avoidance rules so he must be careful not to trigger unnecessary tax liability. He decides to sell the rights to his books to an offshore company in a low tax country that has a number of tax treaties with those countries with which he does business. With careful planning and some able guidance, his books are printed for his company in a high tax country, which then pays royalties to the offshore company with only a minimum withholding tax on the royalties. He has even found a way to have some of the income paid to his company at home (a high tax country) tax free!

The Reality

If William scores a hit with one publication and sells a million of them for $9.95, his costs of marketing and distribution on the Internet could be less than ten percent, for a net income of $9,000,000. Considering that the Internet is projected to have in excess of two billion users in three short years, this possibility is not all that far fetched. What if William were to sell the rights of his publications to a company in Barbados which would have the books printed and distributed by a company in the US to customers around the world?

Barbados taxes individual and corporate income at 40% so it can't be classified as a 'no tax' tax haven. However, international income is taxed at a rate of 1% to 2.5% in Barbados. A number of favorable tax treaties offer benefits for a Barbados International Business Company (IBC) doing business with high tax countries. The withholding tax on royalties paid to a Barbados company by a US corporation is 5%

So, as long as he does it all above board, he will save himself literally millions in US tax. This is a way many major corporations around the world structure things. If William tried this under Australian tax law he would have a few problems, if he had control of the company or had a beneficial interest in say the form of a shareholder. It would definitely come in under the FIF legislation.

- **Example 5 – Investors**

The Story

John and Helen are investors living in Queensland, Australia. They would like to invest offshore to take advantage of several excellent investments that they have discovered. However, they are not allowed to invest with these companies and the reason why? Because, they reside in the wrong place. Yes, they are Australian residents and this is

The "How To" of Global Investment

a disadvantage when it comes to investing offshore. This is due to a number of reasons:
1. Many companies don't bother registering a prospectus here due to the size of our population. Simply, there's not enough money to be made here.
2. Our "red tape" is highly restrictive and onerous.
3. We are a very high taxing country and this would make local operations of many investment companies very expensive to operate.

So, what can John and Helen do? They really want to invest because the potential and past returns are very good and the company is highly respected? The only thing they can do is to invest through an "offshore entity".

The Reality

Firstly, John and Helen can invest offshore as there are no restrictions where they put their money. However, they have been hamstrung by Australia's restrictive practices and this forces investment managers who don't have a registered prospectus and offices in Australia, to deny giving John and Helen the information. Not to be denied, they setup an offshore company in say Vanuatu to use as an "investment vehicle". Still no laws have been broken. As nearly all fund managers have no trouble in dealing with Vanuatu companies, the information and application forms can be sent to their agent in Vanuatu, who then send them on to John and Helen in Queensland. They fill them out in the name of the Vanuatu company and become investors, where previously they had been denied entry. Still not a law breached anywhere.

They do well with their investment and it's now tax time. This is quite simple. If their interest in the Vanuatu company (FIF) is less than AUD$50,000 (including the capital and accrued profit) then they are exempt from the rules and as long as they have not repatriated any income they are tax free (for the time being) and their money can accumulate happily at a rate of knots. If it is over AUD$50,000, then they must pay tax at home on any income that has accrued on their investment. At this time they can also claim any foreign tax credits accumulated by the fund (if applicable). They can also repatriate their capital at any time, tax free, thus reducing their threshold to possibly being under AUD$50,000. However, when a dollar more than their original capital investment is repatriated, every dollar after that is taxable on repatriation. Is this one of the "loopholes" I was discussing earlier when talking about the "British Approach"?

The Offshore Investment Guide

> The important thing to remember is to keep your tax affairs clean as a whistle and that way you can sleep at night. It doesn't mean you can't invest offshore, it just means you still have some obligations. Tax Evasion is a crime – Tax Minimisation is smart!

Strict Rules

Many high tax countries (Canada, US, Australia, etc.) have adopted strict anti-avoidance legislation designed to curb the use of tax havens or Offshore Financial Centres (OFCs) for tax avoidance. It is important to note that tax havens were, in effect, created by high tax countries such as the UK and the US in an effort to reduce aid to certain 'have not' Caribbean and other under privileged nations around the world by creating incentives for multinational corporations to invest. These incentives were not intended to encourage individuals to move assets to these nations in an attempt to avoid paying tax, but that has been the net result.

> Those in business can still benefit from tax breaks or deferrals derived offshore. For the rest of us, we should be content with all the other opportunities and advantages offshore investing can offer with possibly a minor break here and there.

However, companies legitimately established that foster world trade and investment in certain "developing" countries derive substantial benefits from such incentives when they know the rules. Merely setting up a company in a tax haven will not alleviate nor reduce tax liability for the individual in many cases. However, those in business can still benefit from tax breaks or deferrals derived offshore. For the rest of us, we should be content with all the other opportunities and advantages offshore investing can offer with possibly a minor break here and there.

As you can see from the offshore investments I quoted earlier, if you are earning those returns, who cares about tax anyway? You are doing so much better than everybody else anyway.

The decision to utilise Offshore Financial Centres is one that must be given careful consideration. However, if tax avoidance is the primary motivation, a number of obstacles must be expected, by both the

The "How To" of Global Investment

individual and corporation. If, on the other hand, your goal is to access new markets, take advantage of business and investment opportunities unavailable at home or to protect assets from future frivolous litigation, an investment in an OFC could reap untold future rewards, should be considered.

General Issues in Relation to Australian Tax

In general, Australians have a liability to pay tax on their worldwide income. However, there are some differences you should be aware of.

Withholding Tax

When investing offshore you will notice that when a dividend is paid withholding tax is withdrawn from your payment. This is usually 15% but can vary. This deduction however is recouped by claiming it as a Foreign Tax Credit on your tax return. The amount you must show on your tax return is the gross amount ie. the net dividend + withheld amount.

Australia also employs this scheme to investors who invest here but have dividends sent to them.

Withholding tax, foreign tax credits should be converted to AUD$ when you convert it here.

The ATO is **NOT concerned** about these dealings in tax havens:
- Ordinary Trade
- Tourism
- Financial Business including investment
- Private transactions with businesses or people in tax havens
- Inherited money
- Earnings from offshore employment
- Non-residents sending money to Australia
- Former Non-residents bringing back money accumulated offshore

The Offshore Investment Guide

Capital Gains Tax (CGT)

When you make capital gains on offshore investments, they are treated the same way as CGT is treated in Australia and should be included as assessable income. If the assets were originally purchased after 21 September 1999, you will only have to pay half the tax you would normally pay on normal income. So, in effect, if you made a $1,000 capital gain, you only pay tax on $500. Not a bad deal eh? Although you must have held these assets for at least 12 months, otherwise you pay tax on the lot.

CGT on managed funds do differ a little, in that between 21 September 1999 and 1 July 2001, they only receive a 25% discount. In other words, you pay on 75% of your capital gain worldwide. This only applies to managed Funds and nothing else. It's officially called the Cost Base Adjustment.

The ATO IS concerned about these dealings in tax havens:
- Schemes to avoid or evade tax
- Exploitation of secrecy laws to evade tax
- Creation of false deductions in Australia
- Non-disclosure of interest received on Offshore accounts
- Use of debit or credit cards to repatriate "tax-free" funds

---

There is a snag in the CGT thing though.............

Controlled Foreign Company Rules

Probably the best way to deal with the various anti-avoidance provisions currently in force in Australia is one at a time. So we will start with arguably the most vicious. CFC provisions in Australia (as everywhere that they exist) are designed to prevent Australian resident entities from sheltering their income, gains or profits from Australian taxation by locating them in a low tax country where they would be taxed lightly, if at all. To counter this, the CFC provisions impose tax on the resident shareholders of the foreign company on the accrued profits made by

The "How To" of Global Investment

such companies, whether that profit is distributed in Australia or not. This is known as the attribution process.

However, the rules only apply to shareholders who have either 'strict control' (where 5 or less resident shareholders own or control an interest of more than 50% in the company), or 'de facto' control (where 5 or fewer resident shareholders, while not holding more than 50% of the company, effectively control the company by other means).

The income, which is attributed to the Australian resident shareholders is known as 'tainted income', although what is meant by this depends on the country in which the CFC is located. Broadly speaking, there are three categories of countries to which the CFC rules may be applicable. These are:

1) Broad-exemption listed countries. There is no attribution of income for these countries, except where a company has taken advantage of a specific tax concession, and doesn't satisfy the active income test (whereby the company's income is predominantly derived from active business). Broad exemption listed countries include the United Kingdom, Canada, France, Germany, Japan, New Zealand, and the United States.

2) Limited-exemption list countries. This category includes all other countries with comparable tax regimes to the Australian system, and there is attribution of all income for these countries unless the active business income test is satisfied.

3) Unlisted countries. This includes all other countries that do not have comparable tax regimes to Australia, and usually encompasses low tax jurisdictions. Unless the active income test is satisfied, there is attribution of all income for these countries.

The extensive tainted income provisions ensure that CFCs with passive income such as rental income or interest payments will be subject to accruals taxation even where the controlled foreign entity is resident in a broad-exemption list country.

Transferor Trust Rules

These rules exist to prevent Australian resident entities from sheltering assets from Australian taxation by diverting them to non-resident trusts, for example in low or no tax jurisdictions. Where these rules apply, the non-resident trust estate is deemed to be Australian for taxation purposes, and is included in the assessable income of a resident transferor. The categorisation of countries is similar to the CFC rules. In broad-exemption countries there is no attribution of trust income derived

The Offshore Investment Guide

from that country except where the trust has taken advantage of certain tax concessions, and in limited-exemption countries, the net income of the trust (less any amounts already being assessed in the hands of resident beneficiaries) is counted as attributable income and taxed accordingly.

There are, however, amnesty provisions for the winding up of trusts established prior to commencement of Australian residence (where they would otherwise be subject to Transferor Trust rules). Under these provisions, trust distributions to Australian residents are taxed at 10%, and an indemnity is offered to ensure that trust distributions made under the amnesty do not get the taxpayer in trouble with the ATO! However, such an amnesty is only offered once the taxpayer has satisfied the authorities that:

- The foreign trust has been wound up;
- A full distribution of all the property held in the trust has been made;
- That property includes the balance remaining:
- of all amounts transferred to the trust prior to the transferor becoming a resident (or prior the commencement of transferor trust measures)
- of all income derived by the trust from those transferred amounts, or from the reinvestment of such income
- If full distribution was not made to Australian residents, no Australian resident has any direct or indirect interest in that part of the property that was distributed to non-Australian residents.

Easy, isn't it?...ahem.

Foreign Investment Fund and Foreign Life Assurance Policy Rules

Australia's Foreign Investment Fund (FIF) rules apply Australian income tax to the increase in value of non-controlling holdings in overseas trusts and companies if their income is mainly passive, which neatly scoops offshore and foreign mutual funds and other similar types of investment into the tax net. An equivalent rule applies to Foreign Life Assurance Policies (FLP).

However, in June 1999, the government had a partial change of heart, perhaps recognising the tension between trying to ensure that revenue was not leaking overseas, whilst trying to ensure that Australia remained competitive in an increasingly globalised investment world. As a result of this recognition, they decided to exempt interests held in certain US funds from the existing FIF provisions, reasoning that this move would: 'Encourage Australian fund managers to make their

The "How To" of Global Investment

operations internationally competitive by exposing them to competition from US funds, and facilitating portfolio allocations to such funds.'

The underlying message here seems to be that the government realised that Australian resident investors were being unduly restricted in their ability to diversify their portfolios by the Foreign Investment Fund rules, and that they were not necessarily investing in home grown funds because they performed any better, but because they were afraid of the heavy tax compliance burden and harsh taxation pertaining to an overseas investment.

There are several other exemptions from FIF and FLP taxation, including one for residents holding a temporary work permit (i.e. planning to be resident for less than 4 years). Investments totalling under AU$50,000 are usually also exempted.

Foreign Investment Funds (FIF) Legislation

These measures have often been described as "Advanced CGT". This is because if you have an interest in an FIF that is greater than $50,000, then any capital gain that has accrued to investments of the company and will attract tax in Australia even though you haven't sold the asset and repatriated the money here.

The legislation was designed to tax the income of Australian's offshore interests in foreign companies and trusts, that hasn't been distributed or repatriated.

The CGT part of the legislation does not include land, intangibles, plant, inventory, debt instruments, patents or copyrights. Nor does it include companies regarded as "active". Entities involved manufacturing, construction or retailing for example are exempt from the FIF legislation. Companies that are regarded as "passive" and that are very much caught by the laws, are entities involved in Banking, investing, real estate, insurance and finance. To qualify as exempt under the "active rules" your company must use at least 50% of its assets for an "active" activity or be listed on a recognised stock exchange. There are a few other ways to be regarded as exempt, such as if your company owns shares in a foreign bank and that bank's shares are listed on a stock exchange, this investment will be exempt. Also, an interest in foreign life insurance or general insurance company will be exempt under certain conditions.

The Offshore Investment Guide

The Good News

There is an exemption for an interest in a Foreign Investment Fund (Offshore company or Trust) of $A50,000 or less. A small investor exemption is provided for both direct and indirect interests in FIFs. The exemption is only available if you are a natural person and your interest, together with those of your associates (any family members, business partners and related entities), in FIFs, and resident public unit trusts is $A50,000 or less at the end of the financial year. [SECTIONS 96A and 515 of the Income Assessment Act]

> **You can escape the FIF Legislation and its Capital Gains Tax on unrealised investments by simply declaring them "trading stock"**

So, the bottom line is, if your interest in the offshore company at 30 June is AUD$50,000 or less, then you do not come under the tax legislation and can therefore take advantage of the exemption, by deferring tax until another time, letting your investment to grow without taxation, albeit temporarily.

You can also get an FIF exemption if your interests in a FIF are treated as trading stock. The exemption only applies if you elect under the Tax Act to value all interests at their market value each 30 June. This is irrevocable and should be done when you first lodge a return in respect of your FIF income. This means you don't have to pay tax on capital gain you haven't realised, but you will pay tax when you buy and sell investments. In my opinion this would be the way to go as you can actually pay the tax with cash you actually have because it's only on realised profits, not unrealised capital gains.

If you need more information, check out the chapter on Tax in 'The Invisible World', as I go into far more detail there or contact the ATO and request a copy of their "Foreign Investment Funds Guide".

Things that Just Won't Work Anymore............

Now, that there is a major clamp down on illegal activity as far as tax havens go (the legal stuff is still ok), there has been clarification from the ATO what is acceptable and what is not. In the past it was never really clear what was, when it came to some of these schemes. In some cases it still isn't until tested, but let's err on the side of conservatism.

- Offshore loans whereby you borrow money from "a finance company" and claim the interest as a deduction on your tax. The ATO will be looking for any money you transferred to the

The "How To" of Global Investment

company in the first place. They will claim that you are "associated" with the company and knock back your claim. They will also look for any debit or credit cards linked to the company.
- Self-managed super funds that have investments in an "offshore company". Some smarties have dropped their money into the offshore company, received the local tax benefit and deduction and then used a debit card to secretly "clawback" their money before retirement...... Naughty..... and illegal!
- Send your local income (usually in the form of cheques) to an offshore account and claim the funds don't exist hence by-passing the whole system. I always thought this was a dumb idea.... Was never going to work! Cheques are always returned to the bank of issue.... Austrac.... Remember?
- You receive funds in Australia as a loan from an "offshore company", and claim it's not income but a loan and therefore capital. Unless you can prove it is capital...... the ATO think it's a dividend...... tax time!
- Buying a product or service from an "offshore company" at a price that is "a little high" and claiming it as a deduction on your tax. All the time accumulating a cash cache offshore.... Sorry no can do!

There are few other things they are looking at as well, Financing and Captive Insurance, my view is that they won't be nearly as successful here as they were with the blatant schemes above

Money laundering may be out of control, but.............

I read that about every four seconds Australia's financial intelligence watchdog, Austrac, receives details of a transaction involving money either leaving or entering the country, adding to a vast bank of information being used to track billions of dollars flowing around the world.

However, it could still be missing a much bigger picture as age-old guile and the latest technologies are used to evade the barriers erected to stop tax cheats and money launderers. Critics such as Elik Szewach, chief executive of Regis Controls, a company that works on casino technology, believes the bad guys are running rings around the Government's efforts. "There are countless ways of getting around their controls," Mr Szewach says.

The money transfers needed to keep the global economy pumping are mixed in with a vast pool of illicit funds from drugs, fraud, terrorism and tax evasion attempting to be laundered through the economy. It takes a lot of guesswork and the world's top economic officials believe the

The Offshore Investment Guide

amount of illicit crime sourced money could be more than AUD$1 trillion a year, with Australia accounting for at least AUD$3.5 billion. Who knows it could be much higher than this figure, there really is no way of knowing.

> About AUD$3.5 Billion of illicit funds travels through Australia each year and very little is ever uncovered

Austrac admits the difficulties are formidable but believes the "good guys" are winning the fight against the money launderers and tax cheats. However, critics claim the safeguards have become increasingly obsolete as internet, private banking and opportunities provided by casinos create options for washing the cash or getting it out of the country. The volume of transactions is massive and Austrac simply do not have the resources to battle what is obviously a growing problem.

Money laundering is the process by which illicit money earned through drugs, fraud or other criminal activity is introduced back into an economy and used for legitimate purposes. Globalisation has allowed illicit transfers to be totally buried under the weight of a massive number of legitimate transfers. During the past eight years, Austrac's database of suspicious transactions, cross-border currency transactions, cash transactions of more than $10,000 and international telegraphic transfers has increased from fewer than 20 million reports to more than 65 million.

What's reported to Austrac?

- All cash transactions of $10,000 or more
- Suspect transactions where tax evasion of criminal activity is thought to occur
- International Funds Transfers of any amount. Any wire transfer is reported.

It recently revealed that at least $5.01 billion flowed out of Australia in the 2002 financial year to 41 countries identified as tax havens, such as Bermuda, Jersey and the Cayman Islands. Most of money has gone to major banking destinations, and this would obviously include Australian banks transferring funds on behalf of clients, and behalf of themselves as well.

The Tax Office has denied that Australia is losing the money to foreign tax rorts, arguing that much of the money flowing to tax havens is used for legitimate purposes, such as investment. Of course under the FIF legislation and normal business practices much of this money will still attract tax. Transfers to "tax

The "How To" of Global Investment

havens" by major businesses have been undertaken for years and will continue to occur. It's hardly likely that Mums and Dads have sent $5 billion out of the country to avoid tax.

That claim is now (2004) being put to the test as about 1000 of Australia's wealthiest citizens are being asked to provide additional details on payments or transfers of funds into and out of the country.

Tax experts claim closer co-operation between Austrac and the Tax Office has enabled the financial intelligence agency to create increasingly sophisticated profiles of not only where money is going, but who is sending it and when. It is believed that the Tax Office has analysed the bulk of the transfers to tax havens each year, enabling it to look at individual transactions. Of course this only works if someone is silly enough to send money straight from their account to a "tax haven" account.

However, people are becoming more sophisticated in their approach by using "passthrough accounts". This is where a bank account is established in say the UK, Portugal or any other OECD country, and the money is first transferred there and then onto the final destination. This could mean that Austrac could be then tracking down 85 million transactions or even 100 million in time.

It's interesting looking at what the ATO has been presented with when it comes to transactions reported by Austrac. Reviewing the February 2004 edition of "Tax Havens and Tax Administration" report put out by the ATO, it seems most transactions to tax havens, by their own admission are legitimate and relate to trade and investment and this what this book is all about, offshore investment.

Again, like the tax office, they will have to employ another 500,000 people to get it under control. At this rate everybody in this country will be working for the government trying to enforce laws to stop people committing crime. I wonder how that will work? Will anybody actually be doing anything meaningful for our economy?.... Sorry, me just being a cynic again.

A lot of the money that officials are trying to trace, is believed to have been placed offshore into trusts during the seven years between when the Hawke government lifted capital controls in 1983 and the imposition of new controls in 1990. It's believed efforts are being made to trace those trusts by tracking money intended as "tax-free top-ups". So, if you are one of those people, I would be looking to come clean or move yourself into a more legitimate situation elsewhere.

The Offshore Investment Guide

So, You Are Getting Some Tax Advice......................

Tax advice takes two forms.

The First Form is Standard Tax Assistance and Preparation:
One is assistance with the taxpayer in calculating tax liabilities currently due and advising the taxpayer on his obligations and his rights. This is somewhere between accounting advice and legal advice. The scope for tax "avoidance", "minimisation" or "mitigation" in these circumstances is limited indeed. This is tax advice that most of us are given. It is safe, boring and unimaginative. Also, it's given after the fact, once the damage is done. We all hope that our accountant can come up with something a little better but he or she never does. Ho-hum.

However, anything else that results in the taxpayer paying less in the way of taxes than he otherwise should is likely to involve either negligent advice or tax evasion. This is unfortunately the truth.

The Second Form is Tax Planning Advice:
All tax planning takes the form of advising on ways to avoid incurring a tax liability in the future. It is advice on maximising output (after-tax returns) for a given input (income, gains or wealth generally).

This when you learn of better ways to arrange your affairs in a legal and correct way, that will reduce your tax liability in the future. In the first Form, there is only so much that can be done before "legal lines" are crossed and crimes committed. Planning, is a must if you are to reduce taxes in the future.

What is "Avoidance"?

A person can lawfully "avoid" obligations of all kinds. A person fearing conscription may choose to become a citizen of another country. A person wishing to avoid death taxes in country that has them may make lifetime gifts of his assets (although that may involve incurring gift, capital transfer or other taxes). The important point is that "avoiding" incurring liabilities or obligations is a lawful activity, although it may sometimes be considered immoral. However, whether it is moral or not depends where you "stand" in life. We all have differing opinions as to what is right and wrong. I believe taxation is right..... but I believe that the level at which I'm taxed is wrong, as is the way it is spent. That is my call on it, but I'm sure there are some who would disagree..... anybody?....... anybody?

When it comes to taxation, a citizen or resident generally feels a moral

The "How To" of Global Investment

obligation to contribute to the cost of public services from which he or she benefits.

From a legal standpoint, a citizen, resident or other taxpayer is obliged to pay the taxes that are legally due from him. In an ideal tax system the legal and the moral would exactly coincide. But they do not. There are some people who satisfy their tax liabilities and obligations, yet who are considered not to be making the contribution to society that morally they should. As an example: media magnate, Kerry Packer. This is the type of person who "avoids paying their taxes" legally and who (and whose advisers) are subject to criticism by "do-gooders", in particular, socialists.

Then there are those people who feel that their legal obligation to pay taxes far exceeds their moral obligation to contribute. Some of these people see themselves as morally entitled to "evade" their taxes - especially if others are already doing so. These people are generally flaunting the system, and breaking the law. They will end up in trouble eventually unless they are very sneaky or just plain lucky.

> *"If you pay more tax than you have to, you're a bloody idiot!"*
> – Media Magnate, Kerry Packer

Advice on cost reduction?

It's a curious thing. After all, you can get advice from energy experts on how to reduce your electricity bills - increased insulation in your ceiling, double-glazing in your windows, even switching energy providers. You can get advice on reducing your telephone bills, different bill plans, different companies. Finance? Same thing. Investments, get a better return on your money…. Great! Nobody has a problem with any of those things………. However, get some good tax advice and planning advice and there those who will howl from the roof tops that you are a tax cheat and you are cheating the country of its money!

It's ok to "cheat" a bank, electricity or phone company by legal means, but the minute you don't pay as much tax as you COULD have, and paid as much as you SHOULD have, then you are ridiculed. Remember, when Kerry Packer paid his tax bill, which was exactly the amount he had to pay and he was in the right? Remember, when he said, "If you pay more tax than you have to, you're a bloody idiot!" People called him all sorts of things. All he did was obey the law and was given some

The Offshore Investment Guide

pretty sharp advice on Tax Planning. This allowed him to reduce his bill to the minimum he had to legally pay. What is wrong with that? He still pays more tax in one year than you will probably pay in your life. And do you know how much more assistance or services he gets more than you?.......... Probably less. Who's winning in his mind?

Some people will still focus on the fact that less tax has been paid by someone else. However, the (legitimate) tax adviser generates an economic benefit for the taxpayer and himself. This benefits society generally, in the same way that any consumer whose costs in one area are reduced will have more to spend in another area. Demand in the private sector goes up. But what does the government do? It castigates the taxpayer (and his adviser). Paying less in taxes puts pressure on public services, says the government. There will be lay-offs. There will be service reductions. The sick will go uncared for; the rubbish will go uncollected, etc.; tax rates may have to go up, to prevent gross tax revenue from falling. The average citizen will have to pay more, because you are paying less.

Hey, wait a minute! That is exactly what the electricity company would be saying if we reduce our consumption. Or when water restrictions are on during a drought, "now people are using less water (at their instigation by the way), we will have to put your rates up in order to offset the fall in revenue"". So how is this different? Is reducing your tax bill legally different from reducing your electricity bill?

The truth is that the two situations are much closer than most people - especially those in government - would like to think. Governments are not subject to the discipline of the market process in the way that the private sector is. Once taxpayers feel they are no longer getting value for their tax money, they will start to subject the government to a market-type process. They will engage in tax mitigation and avoidance via planning. They will turn themselves (lawfully) into "reduced-tax-payers".

In desperation they may even dabble in tax evasion, or at least aggressive tax avoidance schemes. The government will react.

Illegal tax evasion is often no more than an attempt to subvert a monopoly. It is essentially a "black market" process. In many respects, it is a measure of the degree to which taxpayers do not feel bound morally to contribute to the cost of public services - the amount that the law says is due. The existence of tax advisers, legal tax planning, legal tax avoidance and illegal tax evasion are all different indicators that the tax system itself is inefficient and inequitable.

The "How To" of Global Investment

To some degree, the offshore world has caused onshore governments to re-examine their tax codes. In the UK in 1979 the highest marginal rate of income tax on earned income was 98%. Rates like that are unthinkable today. In Australia, tax rates have constantly been dropping even though there still is argument, and rightly so, about "bracket creep" and the GST cleaning us out again.

To put an end to all the tax stuff (which must be getting boring by now), we can only effectively reduce or minimise taxation by sensible and knowledgeable tax planning, not by illegal tax evasion. The offshore world can assist the investor with many sensible and legal options, but illegal tax evasion is not a smart option.

You Invest Offshore, but the ATO suspects something's not right......

They look at situations where:
- Your Austrac detected transactions don't seem to correlate with your income on your tax return
- You have offshore transactions but have no "Foreign Source Income".... Curious?
- You have money going offshore, but you no longer lodge a tax return..... Why?
- You earnings from offshore, but you don't claim them as exempt?

All these situations will raise a Red Flag, it doesn't mean you've done anything wrong....They're just curious ☺

Are You Liable to Taxation in the first place?

A common question is, "How do I escape taxation at these levels?" My answer is always become a Perpetual Traveler (PT) is a sure fire way. This means, to stop taxation, you have to stop being a resident, because it is residency that determines your tax liability in Australia.

So, are you a resident and how do you stop being one..... read on:

Individual Non-Resident Taxation

A person is resident in Australia if any of the following situations apply:
- He is domiciled in Australia and does not have a permanent and indefinitely continuing place of abode abroad.
- He is not domiciled in Australia but has been in Australia either continuously or intermittently during the fiscal year for 183 days or

The Offshore Investment Guide

more (unless he can satisfy the Commissioner that his usual place of abode is outside Australia and that he does not intend to take residence up in Australia and does not intend to live in Australia for more than 2 years).
- The resident goes abroad to work but his term of employment abroad is less than 2 years and he intends returning to Australia
- Other factors to be taken into account and which alone or in combination indicate Australian residence are
  o The individual's permanent home is in Australia
  o The individual's habitual abode is in Australia
  o The individual's closest personal and economic ties are in Australia

Non-residents are taxed on income "sourced" in Australia, including the following situations:
- The income was earned through a branch or permanent establishment located in Australia and owned by the non-resident individual. Permanent establishment normally denotes a physical presence of more than 6 months in the fiscal year.
- The income was earned from a contract accepted by an Australian agent authorized to accept contracts on behalf of a non- resident principal. Thus although the principal is non resident it is the resident agent who accepts the offer meaning that the contract is made within Australia (since under Australian law the place where the contract is accepted is the place where the contract is made). Where a contract is made within Australia, the income is deemed to be sourced, from within Australia, for tax purposes. (If the resident agent only sought out customers and it was the foreign principal who negotiated and executed the contract then the contract would have been made outside Australia and so for tax purposes the source of income would be outside Australia).
- A combination of some or all of the following circumstances applied to the contract executed by the non resident:
  o The contract for services was signed in Australia
  o The contract for services is to be performed in Australia
  o Australian law is the implied or express proper law of the contract
  o Australian currency is the currency of payment
  o One or both of the parties to the contract resides in Australia
- Rental income from Australian real estate owned by a non-resident individual is deemed to have an Australian source and is therefore taxable in Australia.

As a partial exception to the rule, an employee will not pay tax in Australia on his income if:
- His employer is non-resident in Australia, and

The "How To" of Global Investment

- His employer is resident in a country which has a double taxation treaty with Australia, and
- The employee stays in Australia for less than 183 days in a fiscal year

Capital gains are taxed in much the same way as income, but with an up to a 50% reduction in tax that now applies to capital gains, but only on a resident's capital gains, or capital gains made within Australia.

ATO Investigating Foreign Trust Tax Avoidance Schemes, by Mary Swire, Tax-News.com, Hong Kong 16 February 2004

The Australian Tax Office warned last week that it is investigating foreign trust arrangements in a bid to stamp out tax evasion.

Under scrutiny by the ATO are activities, which involve the creation of a trust in New Zealand that agrees to provide staff and other services at cost price plus a mark-up to an associated Australian company. The Australian-based business then claims tax deductions for the cost of these services.

The Tax Office points out that no tax is paid by the trust or its beneficiaries on this service income either in Australia or New Zealand, and has observed that service fees are paid into a bank account controlled by the trust to which the owners of Australian businesses also have access.

Tax Commissioner Michael Carmody noted that: "These arrangements may breach a number of provisions of the Tax Act, including the general anti-avoidance rules," and warned that substantial fines are levied where the ATO's concerns are justified.

The Offshore Investment Guide

Offshore Basics

Frequently Asked Questions in Relation To Offshore Investment

Q- Why might an offshore investment be superior to an onshore investment?
A- The first answer, is, because it is less regulated, and the behaviour of the offshore investment provider, whether he be a banker, fund manager, trustee or stock-broker, is freer than it could be in a more regulated environment. Any regulator in a high-tax country will immediately say, oh, of course, if it's unregulated, then it is riskier. Well, they would say that, wouldn't they?

Q- Who can benefit from offshore investment?
A- Anyone can benefit from the greater returns to be derived from offshore investments simply by choosing to invest offshore rather than onshore. But to benefit from the low individual taxation regimes available offshore, one of two things has to be true: either the individual must have residence offshore, or, for a resident in a high-tax area, there must be an offshore structure which provides legal ways to reduce or minimise tax onshore.

Q- How much money do I need to invest offshore?
A- There is no absolute low limit, but the extra costs of taking advice, opening new bank accounts, phone communication at a distance etc mean that offshore investment is unlikely to be worthwhile for less than say $25,000-$50,000. Still, costs are coming down all the time because of the Internet. Offshore banks will take deposits down to $1,000, but for a personalised 'private banking' service, you will need to deposit $100,000 or more.

The "How To" of Global Investment

Q- Should I use more than one offshore centre?
A- Different jurisdictions have different advantages. Depending on your agenda, you may find it useful to use two, three, four, or even five different jurisdictions in your offshore structure. Using two or three jurisdictions in an average offshore structure is very common for substantial offshore investors - one for the corporations, one for the trust, and one for the bank account. This three-level arrangement allows your offshore structure to take advantage of the best laws of each country and provides the maximum level of privacy.

Q- Is it easy to dissolve an offshore fund structure?
A- Most offshore structures can be revoked or dissolved very easily. Either the corporate documents or the offshore jurisdiction's corporate or trust laws should specify the dissolution procedure. Dissolving a trust usually costs no more than a small filing fee or a few hours of a lawyer's time. If it would be costly to dissolve a given structure, you can simply remove all the assets from the structure, so it has zero value. You can then leave the empty structure to be stricken from the jurisdiction's register - a cost-effective way to eliminate it. Obviously it would be wise to check dissolution procedures before entering into any offshore engagements.

Q- What is a trust?
A- A trust works by taking assets out of the ownership of the person establishing ('settling') the trust and putting them into the hands of a trustee. An offshore trust is simply one based in an offshore jurisdiction and its profits are usually not taxable there. The trustee normally follows the wishes of the settlor. Trusts, which are based in 600-year old English common law, have been in common use for offshore asset protection for nearly 100 years. Unfortunately, the high-tax countries have therefore had plenty of time to defend themselves against trusts, and by now their usefulness has been severely compromised for the residents of many high-tax countries. Good use of a trust can be made with Asset Protection Schemes discussed in this book

Q- What is an asset protection trust?
A- A trust designed to accomplish a number of estate planning goals of its settlor, before and after death, including planning for the preservation of the settlor's estate from a variety of risks which would threaten to dissipate the estate if one or more of the risks materialised. An APT is typically established in a jurisdiction other than the settlor's home country.

The Offshore Investment Guide

Q- Why are investments regulated more than other types of purchase?
A- Regulation covers the avoidance of fraud (to protect investors from their own ignorance or stupidity), the avoidance of money-laundering (nothing to do with bona fide investors) and has prudential aspects, i.e. it tries to prevent investment managers from making risky investments that could lead to loss for investors. Regulators believe that people's savings are so important they must be given special protection.

Q- What is money-laundering?
A- The conversion of 'illegal' money into 'legal' money. Thus, a drug-runner who walks into a Caribbean bank with $1m, opens an account, and the next day transfers the money into a Swiss bank account where he invests it into Nestle shares has 'laundered' the money successfully. These days banks are much more careful about accepting large sums of unaccountable cash.

Q- Is it legal for me to make offshore investments?
A- This depends first on where you live. Many countries, including the US, Canada, Australia, New Zealand, the UK, France and some other EU countries, make it illegal for offshore investment providers to advertise their products domestically. Despite this, generally speaking it is not illegal for you to make offshore investments (although the US is particularly restrictive). You must check carefully with local advisers as to your rights.
It is illegal in almost all jurisdictions for you not to declare the income or gains from offshore investments to your local tax authorities, and in those very few countries with remaining capital controls, to the monetary authority.

Q- What is meant by the terms 'domicile' and 'resident'?
A- 'Domicile' normally relates to the country or state, which an individual regards as their permanent/ultimate home location. A person's domicile is established at birth and this remains until an individual resettles with the firm intention of remaining in that new location.

'Residence' is normally determined by an individual's status at a particular time. The rules vary from country to country, but in many cases presence in a country for more than 183 days in any one year is enough to constitute residence for tax purposes.

Q- What is withholding tax?
A- When a dividend (or royalties or interest) is paid internationally, the country from which the payment is made usually taxes the payment as it leaves, by 'withholding' a proportion of it, usually between 10% and 30%. If there is a double tax treaty between the two countries

The "How To" of Global Investment

concerned, it is often possible to reduce the tax, or to reclaim some or all of the money. Some receiving countries allow the withheld tax to be set off against domestic tax liabilities.

Q- What is a double taxation treaty?
A- An agreement between two countries intended to relieve persons who would otherwise be subject to tax in both countries, from being taxed twice, in respect of the same transactions or events. By and large, most offshore jurisdictions do not have double taxation treaties, since they don't have much local taxation. Offshore jurisdictions, which do have double tax treaties usually cannot use them to benefit investors receiving complete local tax exemption.

Q Why do people "expatriate"?
A - For various reasons. Some people expatriate purely for financial reasons, or because of displeasure with government policies, while others are obliged to leave their country of residence by the nature of their job, or the service that they provide. The duration of the overseas stay, the destination(s) and surrounding circumstances can differ greatly, but the uniting factor is that in the majority of cases being an expat can be financially advantageous as well as culturally enriching.

Q- What are the banking/investment options open to me as an expatriate?
A-As an expatriate, you really have your pick of the investment arena,
A lot depends on the tax regime in your home country, but assuming that you are going to be non-resident for the duration of your absence, then nationals of most countries are in an ideal position, as expatriates, to take advantage of offshore financial services in a tax-efficient way.
In addition, many high tax countries offer attractive investment opportunities and tax breaks for non-resident individuals and entities.
There are many different structures and services of special interest to expatriates, so the determining factors need only be the size of your pocket and your inclinations!

Q- What should I do about banking while I am overseas?
A- Whatever your financial circumstances, as an expat you would be advised to examine the possibility of opening an offshore bank account, in order to take advantage of the tax efficiency and enhanced confidentiality that this provides. No tax is payable on interest arising from money held in an offshore bank account, so even if you are just looking for somewhere to receive funds remitted from home, or have your salary paid into, this has to be a plus.
There are various types of account available to suit your means and needs. These include instant access accounts with credit/debit card

The Offshore Investment Guide

facilities, fixed term deposit accounts with tiered rates of interest, and fixed and variable rate accounts.

In most cases it would also be useful to set up a bank account in your destination country (where you will be living or working most of the time), from the point of view of conducting day-to-day transactions more easily. You could arrange with your employer to have part of your salary or expenses paid into your offshore account, and part into the local account.

Offshore accounts can usually be in a range of hard currencies, but the local account may have to be in the local currency: having two accounts means that if the value of the local currency fluctuates greatly, or if you are taxed locally on money received, then you are protected to a certain extent.

Q- Would offshore fund investment be suitable for me as an expatriate?
A- It would be ideal! Fund investment means that you can choose to invest in a particular class of assets without having to examine the characteristics of each asset individually. Also, if you choose to invest in an offshore mutual fund, the responsibility for the management, maintenance and administration is taken by the promoter, manager and custodian of the fund. There are various options, ranging from the ultra safe to the very aggressive, but the two main categories that offshore funds can be divided into are private funds (longer term investment, usually requiring more capital, but hopefully generating greater returns) and public funds (usually open-ended, so more flexible, and requiring less capital). Always depending on their original home tax regime, many expatriates will be able to receive dividends and capital returns from an offshore fund without paying tax while they remain non-resident.

Q- I'm not interested in investing, I just want somewhere to keep my money safe. What type of structure would suit me?
A- If you have substantial liquid net worth that you would like to protect during your expatriation, and afterwards, then an offshore trust may be the way to go, along with offshore bank accounts. This type of structure is more used for asset protection purposes than for tax efficiency during your lifetime, as many high tax countries now have legislation designed to make offshore trusts at best tax neutral. However, the asset protection advantages, and the enhanced privacy afforded by an offshore trust are useful features. Trusts are still effective as an asset protection tool.

An offshore trust basically works by transferring control of your assets away from you (the settlor) to a custodian or trustee, who will manage

The "How To" of Global Investment

the trust in the best interests of the beneficiary/ies (This can also be you, or any other person, group of people, or entity that you specify). It is normal for trustees to operate the trust in accordance with the wishes of the settlor.

There are different types of trusts for different purposes, and you need professional assistance in selecting the right type in the right jurisdiction. If your home tax regime does not yet have anti-avoidance legislation, and you hope to gain tax benefits from setting up a trust, then you will probably use a discretionary trust, in which the trustees have full control over the disposition of the trust income and assets. You can still be named as a beneficiary, however, and the trustees will still follow your wishes.

Q- What is an offshore company, and do I need one?
A- If you are going to work in a country, which wants to tax your world-wide income, or if you are going to return to your home country to a world-wide taxation regime (quite likely) then an offshore company may be worth considering.

This is another complex area in which professional help is needed, but the use of a company can sometimes distance you from your income sufficiently to provide some taxation benefits. In some countries there are plenty of rules to prevent this.

An offshore company can take many different forms, some of which are not of interest to the individual expatriate investor. However, if you have a large and diverse investment portfolio, or provide a professional service (for example consultancy in the engineering or finance industry), then this type of structure may be of interest to you.

If you are engaged in providing a personal or professional service, you may be able to achieve considerable tax savings by setting up a 'personal service company'. You can contract to supply the service regardless of residence, and the fees earned can accumulate offshore while you work for a low salary in the country where you are taxed. It only works in some countries, and you may have to do something more complicated than just owning the company yourself, if it is not to be 'looked through' by the taxman. Penalties for tax evasion can be very high.

There are, of course, many other types of offshore company that can be formed to deal with the needs of large corporations, or expats with very specific needs.

The Offshore Investment Guide

Q- I move around fairly regularly - Can I use the Internet to manage my portfolio/conduct banking business?
A- Of course you can. Increasing globalisation and advances in encryption techniques have meant that many offshore banks offer online banking services, which are ideally suited to expatriates. There are also an increasing number of exchanges and online brokers that allow you to manage your portfolio wherever you are in the world (industry estimates earlier this year suggested that there were more than 14 million online investment accounts in Europe alone, and approximately 100 online brokers in existence, although few of them yet offer access to a truly international set of equity or fund assets.)

Q- I work overseas and move around a lot, but would like to choose an offshore base for investment with a view to possibly working and retiring there at some point in the future. How do I decide on a jurisdiction?
A- Choosing a jurisdiction that you would be happy to invest, bank, reside and work in, and possibly retire to means taking into account a lot of factors, and you will need to do your homework. However, the following information may help you to decide which jurisdictions interest you initially. First of all, the following questions must be asked of any potential investment or banking base:

1) Is the jurisdiction politically and economically stable?

2) Is the tax regime benign for investments?

3) Are there any changes in prospect, which may impact on your investment/savings either now, or in the future? (A good example of this is new legislation to curtail banking secrecy and/or introduce new taxes now being enacted in many offshore jurisdictions in response to international pressure)

4) Are the professional support services up to a good standard?

5) Is there a good communications network in place?

6) Is the geographical location convenient for you during your expatriation, and will it still be so when you return home, or move on to a different country?
If you are expatriated to Australia, for example, you will have no problems dealing with an organisation based in Hong Kong, but tremendous problems accessing an offshore structure in the Isle of Man during business hours. The increasing use of the internet means that this is less of a problem than it perhaps would have been a few years ago, but unless you particularly want to conduct

The "How To" of Global Investment

your business dealings in pyjamas, you would be wise to take this into account!

So, you have found a jurisdiction that fulfils all of the above criteria. That's the decision made, then, isn't it?

Not quite. Although a particular jurisdiction may be ideal for the type of investment or banking that you have chosen, if you are planning to work there in the future, or spend your twilight years there, you will need to consider many other factors.

For example the tax liabilities of resident foreign nationals there; how easy it is to obtain a work or residence permit; the standard of infrastructure and services; and the general lifestyle. I suggest you get a copy of my book, 'The Invisible World'. This will explain in detail all the advantages and disadvantages of just about any Offshore Financial Centre in the World. As well, I go through many issues not able to be discussed within the scope of this book. It's a great reference guide for Agent's and Bank's contact details, that can assist you.

Q- I'm an expat with considerable onshore savings and a salary payable anywhere in the world. Should I use an offshore bank, and if so, why?
A- Onshore banking is subject to the tax and foreign exchange rules of the country in which the account is held, and depending on the size of your savings, and the tax regime of your onshore jurisdiction, the price you pay is likely to be fairly high if your savings are 'considerable'. Therefore, if you are interested in reducing your tax exposure, and in greater confidentiality, it would make sense to examine the possibilities available to you offshore.

It is worth noting, however, that some countries, such as the US, tax world wide income whatever your expatriation status, so you will need to ascertain the position held by the country from which you are expatriating before making a decision.

Q- If I decide to use an offshore bank, how do I know which jurisdiction is best for me?
A- To a great extent, this depends on your personal and business circumstances (e.g. residence, personal wealth, lifestyle, future tax planning structures, investments, relocation plans, etc). You could pay an advisor to do your research for you, but the chances of finding someone onshore with the relevant skills and a broad enough knowledge base in offshore matters are slim, and an offshore advisor might be less than objective about the jurisdiction in which he/she is based. It seems, then, that the best option is to do at least the initial

The Offshore Investment Guide

research into possible jurisdictions for yourself or refer to my book, Invisible Banking that will guide you through the whole offshore banking thing. There are, however, some general points to be considered:
- Is the jurisdiction politically stable?
- What are the specific laws and regulations regarding banking confidentiality? (Has it set up treaties with other countries/regulatory groups, etc?)
- Is there an adequate communications system?
- Is there exchange control?
- What banking facilities are available?
- What are the statutory compliance requirements?

For specific advice for nationals of Australia, the UK and USA, see the chapter on **Banking Issues** in this book:

Q- How do I open an offshore bank account?
A- The requirements and length of time it takes to set up an offshore account are dependent on the amount you are proposing to invest, and the size of the offshore institution with which you are dealing (opening an account with a major bank may take 4-8 weeks, as it can take this long to check documentation and confirm references).
Although the information/documentation that you are required to give varies greatly according to the institution and type of account, some of the more common requests are for:
- Signature Card
- Notarised specimen signatures
- Notarised copy of passport or driver's licence (i.e. some form of photo ID)
- Bank reference
- Utility bill showing residential address.

This is by no means an exhaustive list, and many offshore institutions do not require all of these documents, or require them in different combinations, but this is normally well documented in their brochures.

Q- How secure is my money? Isn't it more risky to invest/bank offshore?
A- Not if you are sensible, no! It is always better to regard offers and institutions which seem 'too good to be true' with suspicion, as they generally are! You should begin your research with well established institutions to give you a frame of reference regarding industry standards, and regard with skepticism interest rates or benefits which seem 'exceptional'.

Also, check that the reputation of the bank that you are planning to deal with is good (word of mouth, media sources, etc). Finally, bear in mind

The "How To" of Global Investment

that whilst taking advantage of existing legislation to legitimately minimise your tax burden with a reputable service provider presents very little risk, unreported offshore activity for the purposes of tax evasion is risky.

Q- What sort of return can I expect on my savings?
A- The rate of return that you can expect on your savings depends on several factors. The interest which you will accrue depends on the amount invested, the length of time for which it is invested, and the individual institution and jurisdiction. However, it is worth noting that higher rates of interest are a benefit, which does not really come into play in the general field of offshore banking. These can be expected in a private banking relationship involving a very substantial investment.

More of an issue is the currency that you decide to keep your assets in, and the relative strength or weakness of this at any given time. You may decide that it is easier to maintain your savings/income in whichever currency your liabilities are paid, or you may decide to examine the status of the various currencies, and proceed from there. This does not have to be a permanent decision, as more and more, offshore jurisdictions are offering foreign exchange services to their clients.

Q- How do I deposit and get access to my money?
A- Depending on your needs, there are many ways of obtaining access to your money. It can be done by post, courier, fax, telephone, over the internet (IF sufficient security measures, such as encryption capabilities and protection against account losses, due to deliberate interference, are in place) or bank wire transfer. It is also worth noting that most offshore banks will not accept cash deposits, and some will not accept cheques over US$ 5,000 without authorisation in advance.

So, make sure you check this out before you start a relationship with them. However, if you have transferred all the capital you want offshore, and are not still in the process of transferring funds, by far the most convenient way to access your savings is by using an offshore credit card.

Q- How does an offshore credit card work?
A- In a great many cases, an offshore card can usually be applied for at the same time that the account is opened. The majority can be used both to withdraw money from ATM machines worldwide and to pay merchants, in much the same way as an onshore card.

Where onshore and offshore cards differ, however, is that the latter are, for the most part "secured", which means that you are required to provide a security deposit with your application, and you do not have to undergo a credit check. The deposit required depends upon the desired

The Offshore Investment Guide

credit line, but as a general rule, usually ranges from between 125% to 200% of the credit line requested. Many cards offer additional benefits such as insurance, and card/cash replacement.

Q- What is the difference between a secured and an unsecured offshore credit card?
A- Usually a significant amount of your hard-earned money down the drain! The majority of the offers you will find, promising you an "anonymous, unsecured and 100% approved" credit card fall firmly into the too good to be true camp! Drawn by the promise of complete anonymity, the 'low' application fee, and the absence of security deposit, the unwary investor eagerly remits his initial administration fee, and in the majority of cases, this is the last he hears of it. Very rarely do reputable institutions offer unsecured credit cards, and then only to well-known clients with substantial assets.

As the saying goes: 'You get what you pay for' (or rather, you don't get what you don't pay for!) Unless you fall into the above category, you would be wise to ignore the pitches of unsecured offshore credit card promoters, and resign yourself to the idea of providing a security deposit in exchange for a genuine and legitimate offshore card. Only deal direct with the bank yourself or ask your reputable agent for a "bank introduction"...... but you never should have to pay an application fee for a credit card.

Q- Is an offshore credit card expensive to maintain?
A- There are additional administrative and transactional costs to bear in mind, and charges for services such as use of ATM machines can be quite high. The rate of return on your security deposit will also be significantly lower than could be expected for other types of offshore investment. For this reason, offshore credit cards may not be right for everyone, and it is a decision, which needs to be made based on the size of your investment, and personal situation.

Q- What is an offshore debit card?
A- An offshore debit card provides you with the option of accessing savings held in an offshore account in much the same way as an onshore card would. A note of caution, however: obviously, an offshore debit card requires you to transfer funds to your chosen jurisdiction for 'safekeeping'. Choose the location carefully, to avoid communication/logistical difficulties later on.

Q- What is private banking?
A - The expression 'private banking' is more to be seen as a gateway into investment management in the broader sense than as offering a

The "How To" of Global Investment

confidential, almost family relationship with a man to whom you entrust your money.

Those relationships still exist in the traditional places, like Switzerland, but they apply more to extremely rich people (people who don't know how many millions they have) than to moderately wealthy or well-off people (who don't know how many thousands they have). It applies to people who want more personalised treatment than they can get from their high street branch, or their regional 'personal banker'.

In a nutshell, if you have US$100,000 to get started at a bank, you'll get their attention and be offered better services, like private or premium banking.

Q- What is Offshore Asset Protection, and do I need it?
A- "Asset Protection" Does exactly what it says on the label. If you have a substantial net worth, this may be an aspect of offshore private banking which interests you. People are turning to offshore asset protection as a way of safeguarding their savings from litigation, or possible future divorce settlements, by distancing themselves from their assets in the eyes of the law. Offshore asset protection can be achieved in a number of ways, for example the establishment of trusts, IBCs (International Business Corporations), foundations, partnerships, and other legal entities.

There is, however, absolutely no point in attempting to set up an offshore structure for the purposes of asset protection during, or immediately before action is taken against you, as fraudulent conveyance statutes will mean that if your intention is seen to be to defraud a legitimate creditor, your structure will afford little or no protection. See our chapter on **Asset Protection** and you will find out exactly how to go about it and what it can do for you.

Q- Is private banking private?
A- In most countries one of the terms of the relationship between banker and customer is that the banker will keep the customer's affairs secret. Staff members are normally required to sign a declaration to this effect. Where numbered accounts are used, their purpose is to limit the number of persons who know the identity of the client. In certain countries (e.g. Switzerland and the Cayman Islands) specific legislation makes breaches of bank secrecy subject to criminal law sanctions. However, in all legal systems (including Switzerland) there are specific cases where the duty of secrecy of a banker is overridden by local legislation or international treaties, e.g. where fraud, money laundering and drugs are involved.

The Offshore Investment Guide

Q- What is the situation regarding exchange of information between countries?
A- The recent recommendations of the FATF (Financial Action Task Force) and the initiatives of the G7 and EU countries, and the OECD have thrown bank secrecy policy into turmoil. These recommendations have been targeted at jurisdictions, which the FATF considers to have 'serious systemic problems with money laundering controls' and for those who fail to review their practices and make reforms, the adoption of 'counter measures' has been darkly hinted at. The recommendations hinge on creating greater transparency during the process of offshore investment/banking, and the reporting and exchange of information regarding transactions deemed to be unusual.

Q- How will OECD and FATF changes affect me?
A- See our chapter on **Changes to the Offshore World** for a detailed insight how what will and won't affect you. But generally, if you are not committing a crime, it's business as usual.

Q- What is an investment fund?
A- An investment fund is a pool of money contributed by a small or large number of subscribers, unit-holders or shareholders, which is invested and administered on their behalf. They share the proceeds (or losses) in proportion to their subscriptions after the deduction of costs.

Q- Who runs an investment fund?
A- Three distinct functions exist: the promoter is the person or company who established the fund and markets it; the manager is the person or company who runs it from day to day, and the custodian is the person or company who holds the investment assets on behalf of the subscribers. In some jurisdictions, these functions have to be exercised by separate bodies, but in many, two or more can be combined. All three functions are rewarded with fees, usually based on the value of the fund, but sometimes being success-based.

Q- What is a mutual fund?
A- A mutual fund (a unit trust in the UK and a managed fund in Australia) is an investment fund divided into units (equivalent to shares) which can be bought from and sold back to the manager of the fund, but which are not traded as such. The value of the fund NAV (net asset value) per unit is calculated frequently. Many countries have favourable tax regimes for mutual funds, to encourage saving.

Q- What is UCITS?
A- This is an EU Directive which establishes a common regulatory regime for Undertakings for Collective Investment in Transferable Securities, ie funds under UCITS can market themselves throughout the

The "How To" of Global Investment

EU. As the name implies, investments are limited to those securities listed on public stock exchanges. Many mutual funds in Europe use the UCITS legislation.

Q- What is an open-ended investment fund?
A- It is one, which has no pre-determined closing date. Most publicly marketed investment and mutual funds are open-ended.

Q- What is a closed-end investment fund?
A- It is one with a pre-determined closing date, on which the fund's assets must be realised and the proceeds distributed back to the subscribers. Closed-end funds are normally used by groups of private investors, often working in 'limited partnerships' for tax reasons.

Q- What is an offshore investment fund?
A- It is one which is based in an offshore jurisdiction, (although the term is often used, perhaps incorrectly, to describe a fund which is based outside a particular high-tax country). An offshore investment fund may have the problem that it cannot market into some important high-tax countries unless its local supervisory and regulatory regime is 'recognised' by high-tax countries as being up to their standards. Broadly speaking, this means that if you see an offshore fund being marketed in a high-tax country, its investment behaviour is probably quite constrained, and this may limit its ability to achieve high returns, in the interests of protecting investors.

Q- What types of offshore fund are there?
A- Offshore funds come in many varieties, even more than onshore funds, (those in high-tax countries) which are often limited by local regulation to less volatile types of investment. Thus, there are offshore bond funds, equity funds, sectoral funds, emerging-market funds, money-market funds, hedge funds, property funds, income funds, capital funds - and more.

Q- What is an offshore equity?
A- An offshore equity is one that is listed on a stock exchange in an offshore jurisdiction. Usually there are no withholding taxes on dividends paid out, and very low local taxation of corporate profits. An offshore equity brokerage is simply one that is based offshore, and allows you to buy regular 'onshore' equities from an offshore base. This won't directly help you to escape withholding taxes, but it may help with national stamp duties and capital gains tax, as well as preserving confidentiality.

Q- What is a 'recognised' exchange?
A- If a stock exchange has a regulatory and supervisory regime, which is up to the standards of established stock exchanges in high-tax

The Offshore Investment Guide

(OECD) countries, then it may be 'recognised' by the authorities in some or all OECD countries. This means that securities listed on it can be offered for sale in the high-tax countries concerned, and in particular can be bought by mutual funds within high-tax country regimes.

Q- How do offshore equity brokers' rates compare with other discount brokers?
A- Rates are usually competitive against both broker-assisted and Internet brokers, and extremely attractive compared to traditional full service brokers.

Q- How do I deposit securities into an offshore brokerage account?
A- Endorse your securities certificate exactly as it appears on the face of the certificate. Write the number of your offshore brokerage account number on the upper left face of the certificate. On the back of the certificate between "appoint and attorney" write the name of your offshore brokerage's settlement agent (obtainable from the brokerage) which ensures that the certificate can be negotiated only by the agent. Then send the certificate to your brokerage by a secure route, along with your written instructions.

Q- What type of accounts can I open with an offshore equity brokerage?
A - Individual and Joint Accounts (cash or margin)
Corporate and Partnership accounts.
Estate and Trust accounts.
Investment Club accounts.

An individual account is appropriate for investors who will be the sole owner and authorised manager of their investments.

If your account is to be owned by two or more persons, you may want to open a joint account. A joint account will enable each owner to trade in the account and to receive income, proceeds, or securities from the account.

To open a Corporate or Partnership account you must complete a paper application and provide a corporate or partnership resolution.

Trust or Estate accounts require legal documentation in addition to account applications before they can be established.

To establish an investment club account, for a group of individuals trading under one entity name, you must fill out a paper application and provide an investment club agreement.

The "How To" of Global Investment

Q- Can I use the Internet to buy offshore equities?
A- The Internet is becoming an excellent tool for international and offshore investors. If the online investment site is properly structured (with SSL encryption technology and digital certificates, which are common features), it should be both safe and efficient. More and more brokerage firms and exchanges are moving to Internet-based clearing services and online financial services. The Internet allows you to manage your offshore portfolio with the click of a button, from the comfort of your home. This has substantially reduced physical barriers to international investing and allows investors to stay informed and make profitable investment decisions. Offshore investors can also use the Internet to develop their knowledge and understanding of foreign jurisdictions, investment products, and the investing process.

Q- What special tax treatment is given to pensions investment?
A- Governments in high-tax countries apply a variety of techniques to encourage saving towards retirement: sometimes, contributions into pension plans are tax-free; sometimes the investment gains within pension funds are wholly or partly tax-free; sometimes the proceeds of pension plans are wholly or partly tax-free. Nowhere are all three things true simultaneously, but two are sometimes available.

Q- Who can benefit from offshore pensions investment?
A- For a resident in a high-tax country receiving tax breaks on domestic pensions investment, funds built up offshore are not likely to be able to do more than match growth in a domestic fund, and the resulting income or capital gain is sure to be taxed when it is remitted home, and for many jurisdictions, even if it isn't.
However, individuals in many other situations can gain advantage from offshore pension investment, for instance:
- Expatriate executives, professionals or entertainers
- Residents in high-tax countries intending to become non-resident on or before retirement
- Residents in low-tax countries

Q- What is offshore pensions investment?
A- 'Onshore' pensions usually bundle insurable benefits such as payments on death or disability together with pension or superannuation fund contributions as such, for tax reasons. Offshore, there is no point in doing this, and pensions investment means simply building up a secure, tax-efficient fund which can be distributed when and where you want it in future. Buying deferred annuities is another way of achieving a pensions goal - this is obviously very secure, but the rates of return assumed by the annuity purchase are unlikely to be attractive to the

The Offshore Investment Guide

average offshore investor. Insurable benefits can be bought separately wherever they are cheapest.

Q- What is an annuity?
A- A series of annual (or monthly) payments offered by an insurance company in exchange for payment of a capital sum. A deferred annuity commences on a pre-determined date in the future, but the rate at which it is purchased is determined at the beginning of the contract. Therefore, a lump sum can be applied during a person's working life to purchase a fixed annuity on retirement, whatever the movement in interest rates in the meantime.

Q- Can I transfer my pension or superannuation plan offshore?
A - Complicated question! It depends on where you live, the type of plan you have, where you plan to go, when, etc. You need to get specialised professional advice. There are high-tax countries, which permit part or all of a tax-privileged pension fund, or the income flow from it, to be transferred abroad (offshore) in a way which preserves some tax advantages, but it is not easy. In many cases the answer will be yes, but you will pay at least the basic rate of income tax on the transfer. Even this may be advantageous depending on your present and future circumstances. If you are planning to live offshore, it is well worth looking hard at the possibilities for transferring your pension plan.

Offshore Investing Myths Exposed!

- 'Many offshore investments are illegal.' Fact: No Australian laws prohibit any offshore investments, although most are taxable and must be reported to the ATO.
- 'I'm not rich, so I can't benefit from offshore investments.' Fact: You can open an offshore bank account for as little as US$15,000, with easy access to vast investment opportunities, including foreign stocks, bonds and CDs.
- 'I'll be audited by the ATO if I invest offshore.' Fact: The great majority of ATO investigations of offshore investors are aimed at those who fail to report offshore accounts and profits, not those that do.
- 'Australian investments are safer than offshore investments'. Fact: Many international markets are safer than Australia, in fact most of them! Example: The Swiss insurance industry has never experienced a business failure in its 140 year history. Just look what has happened to HIH and nearly happened to GIO.

The "How To" of Global Investment

- 'It's more expensive to invest offshore.' Fact: Many offshore investments are much better cost deals than their Australian counterparts. Example: Purchase foreign currency CDs (Certificate of Deposit) outside Australia, and you receive higher interest rates and pay lower fees.
- 'All investments I want are in Australia.' Fact: Over 97% of global financial activity takes place outside Australia. Offshore markets are essential to diversify investments internationally.
- 'There are no longer any privacy advantages to offshore investing.' Fact: You must report and pay taxes on most offshore investments, but assets outside Australia disappear from the domestic 'radar screen and from business competitors, sue happy lawyers and identity thieves etc ....
- **The fact is, international investing is safer and more profitable than ever, and it's perfectly legal for you to 'go offshore.'**

Offshore for Different Reasons and Different People

There is no one plan that will fit everyone. Everybody is different. They have different reasons for wanting to go offshore. The possibilities of "what to do first" are endless. But my suggestion is to ask yourself.......

"What do I want to accomplish"?

"Am I trying to accomplish...............
- Asset protection?
- Tax minimisation?
- Establishing an international division for an existing business?
- Getting away (physically) from relatives or spouse?
- Making more money in a new career?
- Changing name, passport, and country of citizenship & disappear?
- Starting a new life?
- Doing good by establishing & running a charitable, education, religious, or research institution?
- Having more fun at a playground where your favourite pass-time is legal, accepted, cheap, and always available?
- Living in a palm tree lined tax haven?
- Living cheaply with a lot of servants?
- Having better investment results?
- Escaping a vendetta against you?

The Offshore Investment Guide

- Living in a place where you can flaunt your wealth?

Then ask yourself.............

- Do I plan to leave my home country? Permanently or temporarily?
- Do I plan to stay right where I am and just have a financial presence offshore?
- If you didn't have your present problem, and if you had all the money you needed to live anywhere in the world without working, what would you like to do with the rest of your life?

Obviously, the plan for each person would involve some variations, depending upon how much is available for investment, or your personal circumstances. For example, a person with $250,000 still has to work for a living. However, someone with $20 Million doesn't even have to think about the cost of living factor because he can live well on 7% interest, anywhere on Earth.

Consider for a moment what you are trying to achieve, your goals and how Offshore Investment can help you achieve those goals.

> **You cannot discover new oceans unless you have the courage to lose sight of the binding shore**

The "How To" of Global Investment

Changes to The Offshore World

The Financial Action Task Force

In recent times there has been much written about the FATF and its future impact on tax havens and how they operate. First, I should explain what it's all about. The Financial Action Task Force on Money Laundering (FATF) is an inter-governmental body, which develops and promotes policies, both nationally and internationally, to combat money laundering. The FATF makes recommendations to member nations in order that they can legislate against money laundering and the crimes associated with it. In the context of this book it has little effect in the way the average business person or investor would use offshore financial centres because money laundering is something organised crime and drug dealers get involved in and I trust you aren't involved in any of these activities.

However, there are some privacy issues that the efforts of the FATF has raised, specifically, the right of access to banking records that exist in certain jurisdictions. If this was to occur, and it hasn't yet, the banking records of clients in offshore banks would be exposed to foreign governments and if these people weren't exactly being honest with their government when it came to matters of taxation, it could cause some concern. Of course, this would only apply to people that foolishly did their banking in their own name and not paid tax on any income earned.

If of course you incorporated a company and set up it up correctly, there would be very little to concern yourself with, as the banking records would be of little interest due to the fact that the company was in fact simply a local corporation run by locals, simple as that. In addition, you wouldn't be breaking anybody's laws, and that's the most important thing. Understand the law and use it to your advantage. That is every citizen's right. What is of more concern is the OECD's Report on Harmful Tax Competition.

The Offshore Investment Guide

The OECD Report of Harmful Tax Competition

This is the report that has many so-called tax havens worried. I could go on for pages about this, but it would bore you to tears. What it means in a nutshell is, the 30 OECD nations, which includes Australia, NZ, UK and US all have similar levels of corporate and personal taxations, and they recognise the existence of tax havens means they don't get all the tax they feel they are entitled to. So what they have done is use their economic might to pressure these generally smaller and less powerful countries to give up their "harmful tax practices".

> **Norfolk Island......   where no taxes are paid by Australians**

This is international bullying of monumental proportions and many critics and even supporters believe it may be in contravention of God knows how many international laws. However, they persist anyway. Now, keep in mind the only thing keeping many of these tax haven countries afloat is their status as a tax haven, so this isn't something these governments will part with easily and many have already told the OECD to "get stuffed" and cited international law and their right as sovereign nations to make laws as they see fit.

This is something that will continue for ages and will result in many years of court battles and diplomatic rifts. Already, we have seen the UK weaken as they are brought to task about the Channel Islands, the Isle of Man and others. These jurisdictions have already threatened that they will undertake total independence from the UK if needs be.

New Zealand has the issue of the Cook Islands and Niue. Dear, old Australia has its own problem with Norfolk Island, where no taxes are paid by Australians living there. You didn't know that did you? See, even Australia has skeletons in the closet!

The OECD has named virtually every country in this book as a target but very few have capitulated in the two years this has been going on. Even Australia was named on an early list!

The jurisdictions that have not sided with the OECD are:
  Monaco
  Switzerland
  Liechtenstein
  Liberia
  Marshall Is
  Andorra

The "How To" of Global Investment

Many offshore financial centres have made concessions, allowances or have implemented their own legislation that has appeased the OECD to a certain extent.

So, what do you do? Well, for a start you avoid doing any business in these places if you can, that's if you value your privacy. But, all is not lost. These jurisdictions will only co-operate when they are asked to. That means the information on you must be requested in the first place. Again, it comes back to the situation, you first must be breaking the law and be of interest to your government, secondly they need to know where to find your records, if they indeed even exist, and lastly you need to be doing business in this jurisdiction in your own name. If this doesn't apply to you, what are you worried about?

This whole thing is about corporate tax evasion as well as "big fish". Sure, if they happen to stumble upon you that's ok for them too. However, that is unlikely unless you are guilty of the above breaches. Ultimately, the OECD would also like all countries on earth to have the same tax rates, but this will never happen and most feel they have already given up on this utopian goal. However, any changes to how the average person or corporation can legally use "Offshore Financial Centres" will take years. Maybe it will never happen, which is what I'm hearing and reading, so you may as well get on with your life and stop worrying about what may never happen. As I said earlier, if you set up any type of offshore banking or investing "vehicle" correctly and legally, it won't impact upon you anyway.

Bearer Shares...... Finished or "Immobilised"?

Bearer shares are an integral part of owning an offshore company or an IBC (International Business Company. The bearer share is different from the usual shares in that it is issued to the bearer rather than a registered owner. This made the identity of the owner difficult to determine to an outsider, as the owner was whoever had possession of the share at that point in time. In this way, privacy was assured.

However, the last few years have seen considerable debate between Offshore Financial Centres and a number of overseas authorities and Governments, the OECD and its Financial Action Task Force regarding bearer shares. Most International Business Companies (IBCs) have included in their Memoranda of Association, power to issue bearer shares. The reality seems to be that, only a minority of IBCs actually issue bearer shares. However, the possibility that a large number of IBCs in OFC's around the world may have actually issued bearer shares has placed many of them under intense international scrutiny.

The Offshore Investment Guide

It was no surprise when in June 2000 the Chief Minister of the British Virgin Islands (one of the largest issuers of IBCs) made a commitment on behalf of the government to immobilise bearer shares. It seems many OFC's are doing a similar thing and it won't be long before bearer shares, in the old form, no longer exist except in a handful of jurisdictions. Bearer shares will be required to be held in custody by either an authorised custodian or a recognised custodian.

Authorised custodians will consist of persons who hold a valid licence issued by the government. Recognized custodians will consist of two classes. Category 1 will consist of a selected list of readily identifiable investment or securities clearing organisations or settlement systems that specialize in the custody business and who are specifically designated by the government as recognised custodians.

> In a nutshell what this means is that bearer shares of an IBC will have to be held by either a custodian recognised by the government or must be registered and held by the beneficial owner

Category 2 will be regulated financial institutions anywhere in the world who are subject to Financial Action Task Force, the Basel Committee on Banking Supervision or International Organisation of Securities Commissions customer due diligence obligations and principles, and who satisfy the government that certain safeguards are in place for the secure custody of bearer shares.

The person depositing the bearer shares must provide the custodian with the name of the beneficial owner of the shares, the name of any other person having an interest in the shares and any other information that, may be prescribed. For IBCs that don't comply with the new rules, many governments will have the right to wind up the company after two years of non-compliance.

In a nutshell, what this means is that bearer shares of an IBC will have to be held by either a custodian recognised by the government or must be registered and held by the beneficial owner. For those who believe this is an infringement on financial privacy, there are some solutions to this problem. The first is to have the shares held by a custodian on behalf of a trust, whose beneficiaries are not directors or owners. Secondly, they could be held by another IBC in a jurisdiction, which doesn't have bearer shares necessarily but also doesn't hold particularly complete IBC registers.

The "How To" of Global Investment

Banking Changes

Every offshore corporation or structure needs a bank account. The ability to open that account depends upon the bank's acceptance of the corporate documentation. Already major banks offshore are refusing to open accounts for corporations in jurisdictions, of which they do not approve. This can be expected to increase so that ultimately it will be impossible to operate an offshore bank account for a corporation other than one in an FATF jurisdiction, which is doing business in approved jurisdictions

Most offshore centres have already introduced legislation to prevent money laundering. Those that haven't, have licensing already and are now licensing trust companies and corporate service providers. The requirements of such licences are stringent. The owners or directors of the corporate service provider have to prove that they are 'fit and proper' persons to run such an undertaking. This means police checks, solvency checks, references, CVs, etc., etc.

Typically, a regulated, corporate service provider is required by law to:
- report suspicious transactions
- maintain certain defined standards in record-keeping
- keep basic non-audited accounts for each company

The underlying principle offshore now is 'KYC' – "know your client".

"Know Your Client" Requirements

Offshore banks and service providers are often asked "why do you ask so many questions?" by clients forming companies with us. For example, most rules seek to eliminate any criminal activity, and in particular money laundering. They will always ask for a bank and professional reference on the ultimate beneficial owner together with a suitably certified copy of their passport. This procedure is known as 'due diligence'.

Legislation controlling corporate service providers, also places a great legally-enforced responsibility on them to ensure maintenance of correct records, compliance with regulatory orders and stringent anti-money laundering laws. It is now also a requirement that either the corporate service provider or the client prepare basic accounts for companies under administration.

Normal requirements are now:
- A professional and/or a bank reference

The Offshore Investment Guide

- Certified copy of a passport or driver's licence to verify the beneficial owner's identity
- Utility bill
- Anticipated annual turnover
- Source of funds
- An understanding of the client's activities and type of business

Suspicious Activity – Money Laundering

This is a list of what constitutes a reportable "activity" in many tax havens, since the regulatory changes have come into effect in the last year or so. It is by no means a complete list but it does cover most situations. All banks and most service providers are employing these rules.

Transactions will be reported when:
(a) clients produce large amounts of cash and ask for it to be credited to the intermediary's client money account;
(b) clients seek to use the intermediary's client money account as a bank account;
(c) clients who settle transactions in cash or bearer instruments, such as traveler's cheques;
(d) clients frequently settle significant transactions by transfers from banks, bureaux de change or money remittance providers located in centres known to be associated with drug trafficking;
(e) clients use (deal through or hold securities) companies located in poorly regulated or uncooperative jurisdictions with undisclosed ownership;
(f) clients have transactions that are in their size, type or nature, not in accordance with their apparent standing or wealth;
(g) clients have a source of funds that is not clear and who decline to provide satisfactory explanations;
(h) clients have an approach to investment risk or reward is unusual. (They may, for example, be unconcerned about return or risk when a normal investor would be);
(i) clients behaviour is significantly different from that of the normal investor. (They may, for example, "churn" their investments or indulge in early surrender of life or investment products despite the penalties);
(j) clients request bearer and other securities transferable by delivery and do not wish to have them held in safe custody or within a recognised custodial system;
(k) clients request the intermediary to obtain, in his own name for them, facilities from banks such as travelers cheques, wire transfers, safe deposit facilities for which the client would normally have to produce satisfactory identification to the bank;

The "How To" of Global Investment

(l) accounts are requested, which are said to be "trust" or fiduciary accounts, for which there is no trust deed or supplemental documentation.

Other reportable Transactions will be regarded as suspicious where:
(a) settlement of purchases or sales involves (or appears to involve) third parties other than the investor;
(b) bearer shares (if available) are requested;
(c) bearer or unregistered securities/near-cash instruments are offered in settlement of purchases;
(d) there is excessive switching;
(e) there is early termination despite front-end loading or exit charges;
(f) they become aware that the customer's holding has been pledged to secure a borrowing, in order to gear up his investment activities;
(g) they are managing or administering an unregulated, collective, investment scheme or pooled funds arrangement.

Legislation Changes

Legislation has been or is being enacted in most of the OFCs, and falls into three categories -

Anti-Money Laundering

The minimum standard, dealing with the proceeds of drug trafficking and terrorist activity, exist in almost every Offshore Finance Centre.

"All Crimes" Laws

All Crimes laws exist in many jurisdictions and go beyond the previous anti-money laundering laws to encompass all forms of criminal activity. Suspicious transactions have to be reported to the authorities, including the suspicion that a client may be breaking the law of his own country. Some laws, though, have been drafted to omit most tax offences.

Corporate Service Providers

Tight controls are being introduced on the activities of corporate service providers so that they maintain certain standards and that their activities are subject to scrutiny.

The practical consequences of these laws are that regulation will increase and the questions asked will become more searching. Honest and serious clients will have no difficulty answering these questions or complying with regulatory requirements.

The Offshore Investment Guide

> The use of Offshore Finance Centres for investment and asset protection will continue to flourish

The Future – 2004 Going Forward

The use of Offshore Finance Centres for investment and asset protection will continue to flourish, however............ many of the offshore centres or tax havens as they are known, who do not comply with the new standards will probably discontinue their operations. The pressure from the OECD and the refusal of banks to operate accounts will make it impossible to use such facilities.

It's likely that by 2008 there will probably be only a handful of jurisdictions offshore, maybe 10 or 15 at the most. These will be serious, well regulated countries which have accepted their commitment to the prevention of criminal activity. This of course being money laundering, financial dealings with terrorists, involved with drugs and major crimes.

You may find that companies and other structures may have to be migrated to better-regulated jurisdictions in order to meet the new standards. Money laundering through the use of offshore facilities will cease to exist, if, indeed, it does now.

It's everyone's right legally to minimise his or her tax or to protect assets and there will always be benefits from the use of international corporate structures. The opportunities, though, are becoming more limited and more complex and professional help will often be needed.

A serious and honest offshore investor will have nothing to fear from the "new order" and will still be able to maintain confidentiality and take advantage of tax minimisation or deferral as well as take advantage of what the offshore financial world offers.

> *"Forty seven of the world's top fifty banks are either located or have substantial business presence offshore. So are most of the world's largest companies. To ignore the benefits the offshore world has to offer would be financial suicide for these corporations"* – Matt Blackman

The "How To" of Global Investment

Privacy & Secrecy

"Hide money offshore and the secrecy laws of the tax havens will ensure nobody ever finds out!"

This is a very common viewpoint and quite correct up until a few years ago. Whilst secrecy is guaranteed by law, it has been somewhat challenged in recent times. It still seems to work quite well unless you are using secrecy to break the law, then it could be challenged. Times are changing.

The Offshore World has by and large used secrecy and privacy as its modus operandi for many years, but things are changing. With the onset of new laws and regulations introduced, in so many jurisdiction's due to money laundering and to a lesser extent, tax evasion, the secrecy laws in many places have been weakened.

However, the secrecy regime that remains in many places, is certainly adequate to stop financial prying, as long as your are not accused of serious crime. Once this accusation is made against you, you should expect the information floodgates to open.

When people think of secrecy, they think Switzerland. However, Swiss banking secrecy is not all it used to be. It can be overridden by statutory provisions, that compel the bank to release information. While limited in their scope, they exist nevertheless in Swiss laws relating to bankruptcy, inheritance debt collection. The most concerning are those related to serious crime such as money laundering.

Accusations by another government against an individual will compel Swiss courts to require a bank to disclose all details on somebody accused of such a crime and their details to be handed to the foreign government for further investigation. To be honest this applies in nearly all "Tax Havens" these days.

Now, not too many people launder money, but there are those committing much less serious crime in the form of tax evasion. It has

The Offshore Investment Guide

been said and reported that governments, where they suspect a citizen of serious tax crime, and knowing that in many tax havens this is not actually a crime as far as they are concerned, accuse their citizen of money laundering and thus catch him out for the lesser crime of tax evasion. Cute trick!

However, two things have to happen before this occurs. First, the government suspecting their citizen of doing the wrong thing, must know where his money is hiding. This is not easy without a fairly obvious paper trail. In addition, they must believe that he is worth going after in the first place. They are not going to employ scarce resources to track down your Cayman Islands account where you haven't declared $125 in interest. They have better things to do with their time. Secondly, the offshore courts, which must order the bank to release the information, must be shown proof that there is evidence of money laundering in the first place. This also signifies that you are a serious "player" in the tax evasion game.

> To get a greater insight into each jurisdiction's law regarding secrecy and disclosure, I recommend your refer to my other books 'The Invisible World' and 'Invisible Banking'.
> There is an order form at the back of this book, if you do not have them.

Hiding Money Offshore?..... But, Why & Where?

Firstly, why do you want to hide your money?
- Is it part of your asset protection scheme?
- Do you have family or friends you don't trust and would like to have a "stash" just for your self?
- Are you paranoid about "economic catastrophe" and would like some money secure somewhere else?

The 3 points above are all reasonable reasons why you would want to hide some money offshore and what's more it's legal to do so, for anybody living an OECD country that is.

If your reasons are:
- Hiding it from the government to cheat on tax
- Hiding it from the courts so they can't distribute it elsewhere
- Hiding it from creditors so they can't have it when they sue me or I become bankrupt

These could be all Illegal reasons to hide money. If you already owe money or have a liability and you then transfer the money out of reach

The "How To" of Global Investment

of your creditors, this is illegal. These transaction can be reversed by the courts and this could get you into a lot of trouble.

Once we have established your reason "Why" and we're happy with that we can get onto "Where".

A couple of rules here that may seem really obvious:
- If everybody is doing it, don't do it.
- Hide things in unlikely places. For instance, English speakers will usually patronise banks and brokers where English is the prime language. Not many people will be looking for your assets in an unlikely place. Like Panama, Uruguay, Mauritius and the Seychelles or Israel.

> **If everyone is doing it, it's the wrong thing to do.**

The basic rule is "Hide a diamond in a pile of sand." Or if you still don't get it, try to think independently of the crowd. If everyone is doing it, it's the wrong thing to do.

Publicity and big advertised seminars are the kiss of death for recommendations on places. However, nobody is advertising and holding seminars telling you to go to the Sultanate of Brunei (near Malaysia) and invest there. Have you heard anyone touting Madeira? I am not saying those are the best places, or even good places. But at least if you have an investigator looking into your affairs, they probably won't bother to look for your money in such off-the-beaten-track places. Not unless you have left them a road map by telling potential informants of your intentions.

So, Who <u>Shouldn't</u> You Tell?

First and foremost, keep it a secret from any solicitor, accountant, financial advisor you don't trust implicitly. However, if you happen to reside in the US, you can't trust any of these people including doctors, with your secrets, as under new laws they all have to forego adviser-client privilege, if information on you is requested. This is of course only of concern if you are paranoid about government investigations.

Others, and probably more important than the above in many circumstances are:
- Potential ex-employees
- Potential ex-friends
- Potential ex-wives
- Ex-lovers
- Potential ex-business partners.

The Offshore Investment Guide

- Relatives
- Also, casual and intimate acquaintances and anyone who might sue you or dislike you for any reason like neighbours and clients. In other words .... EVERYBODY!

Investigators Are A Tricky Bunch.....

Private and government investigators are capable of finding just about anything, and the funny thing is, you are responsible for them finding it. They have ways and means to find your assets one way or another, and here are just a few ways they do it:
- Checking passports (and travel agents) for evidence of visits to "high profile" destinations such as: Switzerland, Cayman Islands, The Bahamas, Isle of Man, Netherlands Antilles, and other well known banking areas and tax havens. Travel to these types of areas will surely throw up a red flag, giving investigators a place to start looking for your assets.
- Examining telephone bills (home, business and hotel), fax, and mobile phone records to identify undisclosed business connections and contacts. Pre-paid calling cards can eliminate this risk.
- Reviewing credit card statements to determine who you do business with, where you travel and what products and services you use. These records leave a paper trail a mile long.
- Garbage is often sifted through for information such as statements, invoices, correspondence, and other relevant material useful in tracking your affairs. Use a high quality paper shredder or discard your garbage at another location. This sounds a bit drastic, but what you throw away says a lot about you, and many leads can be found there.
- Compiling a list of parties that you have a relationship with (business or otherwise) by recording the return addresses on your incoming mail. This technique can disclose friends, mailing lists you are on, associates and partners. Try to have mail sent elsewhere, for instance a "maildrop". Such as a private mailbox or an address not in your name.
- Looking into banking transactions and by checking your bank statements, if they get hold of them. Remember these are delivered by mail. Keep your transactions small if you can. Large transactions always create interest as they may relate to an asset purchase.
- Checking private couriers' logs for delivery of special or important letters and packages.
- Land Titles and Deeds. The biggest single source for investigation is the record of property ownership. For example, tax authorities use this source to check who's selling and whether

The "How To" of Global Investment

they paid tax on the capital gain and whether they could "afford" it according to their income declared on their tax return. What's more, investigators look here first because property, being illiquid, can be seized or have a lien placed on it, forcing you to negotiate it being lifted.
- Motor vehicle ownership records. It's very easy to discover that ownership of a luxury vehicle points towards someone doing a little better than they may indicate on tax returns.
- Tip-offs from informants are a big source of leads: Jealous neighbours, disgruntled employees, unhappy relatives, jilted lovers or spouses. It's best to avoid confrontations and conflicts. Avoid telling friends your financial secrets. Never tell anyone personal information that could be used against you.
- Commercial Mailing Lists and magazine subscriptions, club memberships.

I could go into a lot more detail than I have right here on the Privacy and Secrecy "thing", however, if you would like to know much more on this subject I suggest you obtain copies of my "Underground" Series of books, which go into great detail on these subjects as well as many others.

Underground Knowledge 3
Features the Secrets of:
- Foolproof Asset Protection
- Banking in Silence
- How to disappear
- Amazing Tax Secrets
- Superannuation Lies revealed
- Secrets of Great Wealth
- Portfolio Bonds
- Buying property for $50k
- Second Passports & second citizenships
- Aust. Maildrop Guide
- Airfares for "next to nothing"

Things You Didn't Know
Features the Secrets of:
- PT Lifestyle
- Second Passports
- Investing
- Privacy
- Money
- Database Privacy
- Echelon
- Computer Privacy
- the first Cyber Haven and a wide range of other issues important to the investor
- How to hide and Safeguard your assets
- Billionaires secrets

Underground Knowledge
Features:
- Privacy
- Security
- Special Destinations
- Technology
- Privacy Strategies and Tricks of the Trade
- Money Making Strategies
- Government Surveillance and how to beat it
- plus, many more great ideas, concepts and methods to improve your privacy and increase your wealth.

71

The Offshore Investment Guide

Asset Protection and The Nasty World of Litigation

"Wealth Extraction" – The Art of Removing a Person's Heart through One's Wallet

Ah!..... The joys of litigation. Where one person declares, "You have it.. .. and I want it!" J. Paul Getty was once quoted as saying,

"When I go into any business deal, my chief thoughts are on how I'm going to save myself if things go wrong"

This is the essence of asset protection. "When things go wrong", that is when we need it, and value it. It's no use, and too late to act on it when things have already gone wrong. I know from personal experience, that even the people closest to you and the most trustworthy, can turn on you. So, you must protect yourself.

In the US lawsuits are being filed at the rate of one hundred million cases a year. Many of these suits have nothing to do with right and wrong, but instead, are predicated on the desire of one party to extract wealth from another party. In many cases, this equation is not predicated on the desire to extract real wealth, but on a desire to extract small payments as "nuisance" settlements, because it is cheaper to pay than to fight.

If someone slips and falls in a business, or if a car taps their car's rear end, they react like they just won the lottery. If an armed thug breaks into a home in the dead of night, slips on a child's marbles, and breaks a leg, he can sue and possibly win.

Here are some examples that may frighten you into action:

The "How To" of Global Investment

- One idiot strapped a refrigerator on his back and ran in a race. The strap broke and he hurt his back. He sued the strap manufacturer and collected $1.3 million.
- A woman in Texas was awarded US$780,000, by a jury after breaking her ankle tripping over a toddler who was running amok in a furniture store. The owners of the store were very surprised by the verdict, considering the child was in fact the woman's.
- A woman was awarded US$113,500 after she slipped on a spilt drink in a restaurant and broke her coccyx. Again surprise, she was the one who had thrown the drink on the floor during an argument with her boyfriend.

If lawsuits continue at the pace they do today, each person in the top 50% of income earners in the US will ultimately be sued five times. Australia, Canada and the UK are catching up too.

One does not have to lose even one of these cases in order to lose their wealth, simply the cost of litigating these issues can be onerous enough. One solicitor told me if it goes to court you'll be up for $50,000 win or lose, minimum.

For many people the threshold issue in asset protection is: do I need it? Many people believe "this won't happen to me, it can't happen to my business, my family is safe, because we don't do anything that's dangerous."

However, if you are a person that:

- Deals with the public
- Rents properties or you are an owner of a rental property
- Is a director of a company
- Is in the medical field
- Is involved in a "white collar" profession working for yourself
- Is wealthy

You are talking a great deal of risk and as time goes on your chances of being sued, based on the laws of probability, increase. It's only a matter of time.

> **What you need to do is ensure that it doesn't get to court and that you have nothing worth taking in the first place.**

The reality of life is that you don't have to do anything dangerous or negligent; all you really have to do is be in the wrong place at the wrong time. Ordinary people have extraordinary problems. In many cases

The Offshore Investment Guide

these problems are not problems of their own doing, they were simply matters of circumstance.

Once a judgment is made against you have to tell the court everything. Regardless of how unjust the case is. You must tell them what properties you own, about your bank accounts, investments, absolutely everything. They will then place a value on it and then proceed to "redistribute" your wealth elsewhere. Good isn't it?

Now, you may say, "I have insurance to cover that!" Do you really? Check your policy, you may be surprised on how much you are not covered for. Also, if the insurance company can prove your negligence for whatever reason they'll drop it back in your lap. What you need to do is ensure that it doesn't get to court and that you have nothing worth taking in the first place.

Now it has all gone wrong and you have found yourself on the wrong end of a court case and you must pay up. You are known as a "judgment debtor". As such you virtually have no rights, as the winner now owns everything up to the value of the judgment. And heaven help you (the defendant) if you fudge your testimony. If you conceal a safe deposit box with a few goodies in it you're committing perjury, a crime that carries mandatory sentencing guidelines. You could end up in jail!

> **The only legally valid protection is to take careful and legal protective steps before there is even a potential claim against a person or his assets.**

It is all too easy to go around saying it won't happen, but once it happens, it is too late. If money is transferred after an incident or accident, that is concealing assets, this can cause both criminal charges and civil loss of other assets. The law looks at it as stealing the property of the person who is suing, or who may sue. The defendant may think it is his lifetime savings from hard work, but legally he now holds it in trust for the person who has a pending claim.

Presumed knowledge of the possibility of a claim is sufficient to invoke these fraudulent transfer laws. So if somebody moves their money the morning after an "incident", it is likely to come back to haunt them. The only legally valid protection is to take careful and legal protective steps before there is even a potential claim against a person or his assets.

The "How To" of Global Investment

In Australia, and several other countries it takes <u>two years</u> before your assets are truly protected because during this two years, any transfers can be reversed by the courts...... very scary!

Methods to Protect Yourself #1 – Simple Plan

This simple method is for the average person who wants basic protection.
- You have a home and a few investments to protect
- You are in a "risk" category but your partner isn't
- Transfer the house and investments to her or him to reduce your "exposure". There will be stamp duty to pay but this will only be on half the value of the transfers assuming that they are also in your name initially.
- Have your solicitor or lawyer put together a "post nuptial" agreement that on dissolution of the marriage that these assets to be included equally in any property settlement. Generally they will be anyway, but this can't hurt and it gives you extra piece of mind.

Case Studies to Prove The Value Of Asset Protection

Employee Problems

A group of business partners got together for an informal lunch to discuss their work. One of the secretarial staff in the office is asked to go to a local restaurant to pick up an order for these partners. Unknown to the partners, this employee has a poor driving record based on several accidents and many speeding fines. The secretary leaves the building, climbs into their car, and proceeds to pick up lunch. From time to time during her errand she drives at excessive speeds. The employee pays more attention to the radio than to an upcoming stop sign. The stop sign is missed, the car is smashed, and a life is lost. A subsequent lawsuit, one would think, would simply blame the employee for her negligence, but unfortunately this is not the case.

All of the partners are sued as the result of their negligence, in not determining that this driver was, in fact unsafe. More importantly, this driver was on company business, and the heirs of the woman who died now seek retribution from the remaining partners. Their homes, their

The Offshore Investment Guide

investments, their boats, their holiday homes, even their business are up for grabs.

In the court case, several hundred thousand dollars are spent in an attempt to defend this claim. Unfortunately, this case is not settled because the main suing party, one of the remaining family, continues to expect more money to be found, more wealth to be uncovered.

In many cases one of the prime financial elements that is being sought is insurance. In days gone by, insurance was a protector of the family and the business. These days it often acts as a target and will attempt, if it can to pass blame back to the "insured" and absolve itself from the claim. In this case, it amounted to a settlement by the insurance company but the business partners spent small fortunes in legal fees defending themselves (the insurance company refused to pay the legal fees) and they lost much sleep for many months. Is it worth it?

A Nasty Scenario That Will Frighten Many Property Investors

A property investor working for himself,f acquiring properties, renovating them, and selling some and keeping others to add to his portfolio, finds himself the subject of a lawsuit.

The lawsuit is brought by a group of "squatters". These people who have entered vacant property, have set up households, and are living rent free in houses with no electricity, no water, none of the comforts most of us would expect in a home. The people who move in have small children.

These small children eat some the paint coming off the walls in this property. Unfortunately, the old paint contains lead and is very toxic and the children become very ill. Now, keep in mind these people have no right in this property, they are squatting.

This squatting family now brings a lawsuit against the property owner, and he must defend himself in court against this squatter suit. He eventually settles out of court to avoid the whole "legal battle" thing. He must pay for his legal costs, and the squatters are able to obtain free legal aid.

How unfair can it be for someone to enter your property without your knowledge and without your permission, and through their own negligence, their children become sick, and then they turn around and attempt to sue you? To what degree can the system be so unfair?

The "How To" of Global Investment

These are simply examples of what you could call extraordinary problems for ordinary people. The days are gone when only the rich and powerful are the subjects of lawsuits. The days are gone when right or wrong truly become the litmus test by which a lawsuit is either filed or dismissed.

It is imperative that families and businesses today understand that they are at risk and that problems can arise. Asset protection is one solution...... doing nothing in life and hiding under your bed is the other.

Inadequate Insurance

A doctor works all his life to provide competent and effective care for his patients. Surgery leaves the patient crippled. No surgeon is 100% successful, but the jury in the malpractice suit awards the plaintiff $20,000,000, an amount greater than the policy limits for this procedure. The doctor must make up the shortfall of $5,000,000 out of his own pocket. He is wiped out.

> **All assets within a particular jurisdiction are subject to seizure within that jurisdiction, regardless of how title is held.**

The Reality of Asset Seizure

All assets within a particular jurisdiction are subject to seizure regardless of how title is held. It doesn't matter what you do when it comes to transferring "ownership" of assets from one entity to another. They can still be seized if it can be proven (or suspected) that you have a connection or beneficial interest in a particular asset. Simply transferring it won't do, under certain circumstances.

So, it is best to ensure these things are properly protected, where you can, (where possible) so you have some degree of protection and peace of mind. Ways to do this are:

- Place wealth outside your jurisdiction in an entity that is not "you"
- Make transfers into entities with no beneficial interest related to yourself
- Make those transfers at least two years before anything goes wrong to ensure there is no "clawback". And because you don't know when you will have problems, I'd be doing it now.

The Offshore Investment Guide

Methods to Protect yourself #2 – Company Plan

This protection method should be employed by people, whom have their own company, (usually a family business), to ensure protection for the director's assets. It was believed that a company structure provided protection for the business' directors., but this is no longer true, in many cases. The "attackers" will simply by-pass the company structure knowing full well there are very few assets to go after, and go after the assets of the director or directors. The assets of the shareholders are unclaimable, only the directors.

- Decide which of you should bear the brunt of any claims. This person will remain (or become) the director. These days you only need one director.
- The other partner should resign as director immediately, if they already hold this position.
- Shares of the company should then be consolidated and held by the NON-Director person. The "shareholder" should hold no official capacity other than as a part-time worker.
- Ensure the shareholder can't sign cheques etc. This will strengthen your argument that this person has no authority over the business on a day-to-day basis.
- The non-director / shareholder should also be the person that holds the family's personal assets etc.
- In this way the assets are held with the "non-responsible" person
- The director or "responsible" person holds all the authority but none of the assets.

Remember...... this structure must be setup at least two years before you have any problems, to ensure that it's not possible for courts to "clawback" or reverse what you have done to protect yourself.

The purpose of the Asset Protection Scheme is not to test it out in court, but to deter would be litigants from getting that far. Layers of asset protection are deterrents

The "How To" of Global Investment

Methods to Protect yourself #3 – Home Equity Plan

If you are concerned about your home getting claimed in some future litigation, there is a simple way to ensure there's not much to run off with and at the same time picking up some money to invest.

- Go along to your bank or financial institution and apply for a Home Equity Loan. Borrow as much as you can, within your comfort level of course.
- This will mean that, just say your home is worth $400,000 and you have an existing mortgage of $100,000, that leaves you with equity of $300,000. This is the amount a litigant can take off you if successful.
- Now, if you borrow a further $250,000 (subject to your ability to make repayments) your equity will reduce to $50,000. This is all that is at risk.
- However, you now have $250,000 to do something with. You place this either onshore or into our offshore structure that I will discuss in the next section and it will be isolated from any litigant that is after you. Simple!!
- Placing it offshore is a better idea simply because demonstrated returns are better.
- There are benefits!! 1) The amount you borrow could be tax deductible if used for investment purposes 2) Your returns could easily be higher than your mortgage interest rate and you could be in front overall. 3) Your home is protected from litigation (to a great extent).
- However, things to keep in mind..... There are investment risks with any investment, so you must understand sometimes investments go down. Would you be able to cope with it? Interest rates on your home loan may go up, can you cope with this?
- If you find the whole thing unsettling or it's not for you, you can always return all or part of the funds to you and pay off the loan. This would be the strategy if rates start moving up quickly, however, this leaves you exposed again.

Remember...... this structure must be setup at least two years before you have any problems to ensure that it's not possible for courts to "clawback" or reverse what you have done to protect yourself.

The Offshore Investment Guide

An Offshore Asset Protection Solution

The beauty of this structure is that:
- It can be easily set up onshore for asset protection purposes
- When established offshore, it gives you the same asset protection and even possibly better, because the assets are located offshore. It will also allow you to invest offshore, whereas an onshore setup will still have the downside of not allowing you to participate in some investments, due to you residing here.

What you need:

You will need a company to be established as well as a trust. This applies to both the Offshore and Onshore versions of this Asset Protection Plan.

Firstly, a trust is a legal entity that can invest in shares, property, funds - virtually anything. It is controlled by a "trustee". The trustee makes all the decisions on behalf of the trust, such as what it invests in and whom it provides distributions for ie. Beneficiaries.

The trust will hold all the assets in our structure. For example, if you invest in offshore funds and shares, it will own them. It will own them on behalf of the "beneficiaries" who receive income or profits received by the trust. These people are like the company's shareholders, but unlike shareholders, beneficiaries have no say in the running of the trust. Shareholders in a company can remove the directors if they wish.

The company is also a legal entity. It has a director and shareholder or shareholders. In our structure, it will act as the "trustee".

Finally, you will act as the company's director and shareholder.

The structure will look like this:

See next page

The "How To" of Global Investment

> **The Director and Shareholder of the Trustee Company**
> This will be "you" in the structure
> You get to control everything but you own nothing. In the event that they come after you.... they can get nothing!

↓

> **The Company**
> **The Trustee**
> The company manages the trustee and controls everything. As the director of company you have control over the trust ultimately. However, you and the company owns no assets, just controls them

↓

> **The Trust**
> **The Trust owns everything**
> The trust owns all the assets i.e. investments etc and holds them on behalf of the beneficiaries. All the money it makes – it distributes to the beneficiaries

↓

> **The Beneficiaries**
> These people get all the benefits of the trust – they could include you, your children, relatives your spouse

Bringing The Ultimate Asset Protection Plan Together

I should point out a few rules here to the asset protection scheme:

- This structure should be used only to protect assets. Do not use it for business or run any personal business through it. You can use a separate trust called a "service trust", which can use the same trustee company. The reason for this is simple. The only chink in the armour is if someone sues the trust itself.
  This can only happen in certain circumstances and they are:
  1) if the trust is trading or operating as a business. So keep all your business operations in a separate entity not related to this one.
  2) if the trust owns a property that is rented and issues related to the property give rise to a dispute.

This brings us to second rule.

The Offshore Investment Guide

- If you are using this trust setup for properties, it's best to isolate each property in its own trust. That way the only thing at risk is the one property. If you have multiple properties in a trust, and one property goes wrong, then all the rest in the trust are not at risk. While this may seem inconvenient, and a little more expensive, it's worth it.
You still, however, only need the one trustee company looking after all the different trusts.
- Also, before you put the family home in a structure, remember there are capital gains tax considerations as well as stamp duty. So, it may be advisable to leave property, particularly your home out of these structures and employ: **Methods to Protect yourself #3 – Home Equity Plan** shown a couple of pages ago

The Onshore Asset Protection Plan

For those people, not really wanting or requiring the added benefit of being able to use this structure for offshore investing and would like to use this structure for onshore asset protection we suggest you:

Contact:

Your accountant or solicitor. They should be able to do it for you. The cost will vary of course but expect $3,000 - $5,000 depending on how much work they will need to do for your particular circumstances.

The Offshore Asset Protection Plan

Introduction

Anyone with a reasonably substantial net worth could benefit from offshore asset protection, and this financial management strategy will be of particular interest to those working in professions where there is a high risk of litigation, for example doctors, lawyers, business owners, and financial planners, to name but a few.

As discussed earlier, there are increasing numbers of lawsuits being brought, in which the defendant is being targeted not necessarily because of his culpability in the case, but because of his ability to pay. Individuals in the above high risk groups with savings or significant assets, could well fall in this 'deep pocket' category, and risk losing everything if there are not proper protection measures in place.

The "How To" of Global Investment

Although professionals of many kinds are obliged to have liability insurance or professional indemnity insurance, this is becoming more and more expensive due to the increase in litigation (and of course the collapse of insurance companies like HIH). It is also becoming more expensive because of the rising level of damage awards. In many cases, what's worse, is that your insurance may not even cover the full size of an award. Therefore, it is increasingly important to consider putting in place, some additional asset protection measures.

> **Asset protection strategies basically work by making the assets of an individual unavailable, or exceptionally difficult to recover**

Asset protection strategies basically work by making the assets of an individual unavailable, or exceptionally difficult to recover, (and hence potentially more unattractive) in the event of legal proceedings being taken against them by employees, clients, patients, litigious family members or other creditors.

Protection of assets can take a number of forms, and while there are many domestic alternatives, including family trusts, limited liability partnerships and companies, and family partnerships - offshore vehicles, trusts and companies are usually more effective for this purpose, simply because not only are the structures straight forward, but your asset ownership lies outside your resident jurisdiction and therefore out of sight and out of mind. "Clawback" attempts and litigation is made just that little bit more complicated and difficult. This is another great deterrent in the first place.

The trust is the lynch-pin of offshore asset protection; although offshore bank accounts on their own can provide enhanced privacy and confidentiality, they are usually an integral part of an asset protection strategy. Banking secrecy laws in offshore jurisdictions are usually significantly stricter than domestic laws, and unless criminal activity or money laundering is suspected, you can expect that your details will not be made available to a third party. Banking secrecy legislation does however vary from country to country, so you will obviously have to check the situation in your preferred jurisdiction before taking action. Invisible Banking and The Invisible World will help you here.

> **Placing assets physically offshore is great deterrent to litigants..... it tends to muddy the waters further but also make litigation even more costly for the "attacker"**

The Offshore Investment Guide

Offshore trusts and companies can be used separately or together (better together though) for asset protection purposes (usually in conjunction with an offshore bank account). In a trust arrangement, the settlor (the person who transfers assets to the trust) legally gives over control of his assets to a trustee (or trustees), who manages and controls them for the benefit of a beneficiary or beneficiaries (of which the settlor can be one). Although the settlor will usually provide a letter of wishes, detailing how he would like the money to be managed, and distributed, the trustees have legal control over the assets.

Although trusts could once be used in order to "break the link" between an individual and his assets, this is less the case in recent times, as high tax countries have had time to develop legislation forcing at least some degree of transparency into trust arrangements.

> **An offshore company can still go a long way towards providing privacy and asset protection - after all, your creditors first have to find your company before they can sue it.**

If a person sets up an offshore company (usually an International Business Company or IBC) to hold his assets, he will normally be a shareholder in that company and vulnerable to Court action.

However, in many offshore jurisdictions, the agent establishing an IBC (or indeed a trust) on behalf of an individual is not obliged to name the eventual beneficiary, and for this reason, an offshore company can still go a long way towards providing privacy and asset protection - after all, your creditors first have to find your company before they can sue it.

The flaw in this line of reasoning, in many cases, is that you are obliged to disclose the existence of such assets to your local tax man, and once it's on your tax return, the whole world knows about it. There is also plenty of pressure on offshore jurisdictions to change their rules by installing 'know-your-customer' and mandatory registration rules. So the trust survives, and even prospers as the instrument of choice for asset protection.

However, in Australia, the trust even has to be declared if formed. Unfortunately, false information on your tax return can lead to serious problems. So, you must "work with" the requirements of disclosure making sure you don't qualify as someone who must disclose these requirements. An example of this is using the "under $50,000 rule"

The "How To" of Global Investment

where you don't have disclose your interest if the amount offshore is less than $50,000. Also issues of "ownership and control" can be looked at.

In order to ensure effective offshore asset protection, then, you need to establish the structure in a jurisdiction with effective IBC privacy legislation, strong banking secrecy laws, and modern trust legislation. For a detailed examination of these, and other aspects of protecting your assets and doing business in over 40 offshore jurisdictions, read my book, The Invisible World.

Asset protection however is not something that should be attempted when legal proceedings are imminent, or already underway, as any attempt to transfer assets under these circumstances would be considered a fraudulent transfer. This is illegal, and would provide no protection against creditors whatsoever. However, a well-structured asset protection strategy, set in place ahead of time could prove a very effective tool in protecting both wealth and privacy.

If you would like someone to help you establish an offshore asset protection scheme, I can recommend these people. They know what they are doing and have an excellent record of honesty and integrity and they have been around a long time.

Contact:

Eilish Murphy
ICSL Iberia
Gran Via Carlos III
84, 3 planta
08028
Barcelona
España
Tel:+34 93 496 5703
Fax:+34 93 496 5701
email:spain@ICSL.com

This information is provided as general guidance; anyone considering setting up an offshore company or trust should, of course, seek appropriate professional advice from a legal advisor.

The Offshore Investment Guide

Transferring My Assets to The Asset Protection Scheme

As there are no US, Australian or UK laws or rules against exporting your capital, and no filing requirements or other red tape to be dealt with in connection with sending assets overseas, you just do it.

> There are millions of money transfers overseas every single day, mainly related to world trade. Nobody will be interested in your transfer, unless you are on the government's "black list"..........
> Stop worrying, you are not on the list unless you're a criminal... Trust me!

The bank that wire transfers your money to your offshore bank account, (yes, you will need one of course, how else is the whole thing going to operate?) provides an electronic computer report to the government guys, but don't panic! Many offshore writers will panic you at this point, about nasty conspiracies, but this is not entirely true. Unless your name is on their special little list of "narco-traffickers", members of terrorist organisations, mafia, crime boss or known money launderer, no particular notice is taken.

There are millions of money transfers overseas every single day, mainly related to world trade, tourism (when someone from overseas uses their credit card here) etc. They are all logged electronically, ignored electronically, and forgotten electronically. It doesn't matter if you dribble your money out little by little, or if you make one wire transfer of $20 million. What's the best way? My opinion is that it is best to test with a small transfer first. Say $5,000. Make sure the newly opened account overseas will receive your funds without glitches.

If everything is handled well, and you feel comfortable, you can ship out the big money and get it over with fast. Your worry with dribbling is that some of the transfers will go into the wrong account or be accounted for wrongly. If you do 51 transfers, there is 51 times more likelihood of a screw up than on one. The only reason you would dribble it out is because you really do want that extra bit of "muddy waters". This may be the case, if you feel the person who one day may come after you, is vicious and particularly thorough............ those people can be scary!

The "How To" of Global Investment

If you do send it out in little "bites", you won't lose your money if mistakes happen and don't forget, mistakes can always be corrected. But you waste a lot of time and burn up the telephone and fax lines of communication, which means much more chance of attracting unfavourable attention. If the government was looking for a pattern of transfer, and yours just happened to fall into the pattern, it would attract interest. Just something for you to think about.

Any creditor or government agent will be able to find out, that on a certain date, you sent $X out for deposit to your account abroad. Logic indicates that you must have had $X on deposit at a certain bank overseas, if the transfer was from Bill Smith and destined for the account of the same Bill Smith in Andorra.

If the money transfer went to a corporate account (not known to be associated with you), then your creditors or a government agent can't assume that the money was still yours once it reached the foreign shores. Perhaps you bought a house in France and "Newcorp Offshore Holdings, Ltd." a Turks and Caicos Corporation (who got the money in Andorra) was the seller. Or the first stop for your dough in Europe could have been a trust account in the name of an accommodating offshore solicitor, or a so called "transit account" or "passthrough account" set up by your offshore banker or broker to do nothing but receive and transmit money somewhere else.

It doesn't matter very much where your money pauses on it's first stop in the free atmosphere of "Offshore", however, if you want privacy and invisibility, the first stop (certainly if it is an account in the same name you used at home) can be only a transit point. Don't leave it there.

There are other ways to transfer money, in more complicated ways, and they are discussed in Invisible Banking.

"Foundations"
Do They Work As An Asset Protection Vehicle?

Yes!..........If Give Your Money Away!

You may have heard a little about Foundations. It's a legal entity often set up in places like Panama. It's a favourite of some US investors and I thought we could have a quick look at them here.

The Offshore Investment Guide

Foundations, were the favourite entity of America's rich elite, such the Rockefeller family.

They work by giving a non-deductible "gift" (i.e. your assets) to a foreign foundation or non-profit organisation, set up by yourself. Can you do it yourself? Not unless you have some technical training and have a lot of time to experiment and possibly get it wrong. Usually, you will have to be put in touch with one of the few people in that line of work that know the subject. However, they can be expensive to set up, but if you are seriously rich, worth looking at.

Agents listed in my book The Invisible World, should be able to give you some worthwhile guidance if you are interested.

"We are not afraid to entrust the American people with unpleasant facts, foreign ideas, alien philosophies and competitive values. For a nation that is afraid to let it's people judge the truth and falsehood, in an open market, is a nation that is afraid of it's people"
– John F Kennedy, US President

How long will governments allow us to make choices, have true freedom to do with our money what we like, to be able access knowledge that may not be in the interest of those in power?
How long will they allow us to move freely?
How long before certain knowledge is banned?
How long before books are banned, books that break no laws?
How long before we are completely controlled by governments who regard us nothing more than "serfs"?
How long will it take?................ Or do we resist, and tell them what we will or won't do?
Do we tell them to do their jobs and serve the people, rather than serve themselves? Governments and bureaucrats have a lot to answer for? Let's ask the questions now!

The "How To" of Global Investment

Banking Issues

*"I would never bank offshore..........
The bank could collapse............
A dictator could seize power and take all my money....
Anything could happen!"*

This line of reasoning shows a fundamental misunderstanding of how the offshore banking industry operates. The money (apart from small change) is never in the "offshore country." If it is US dollars, it is on deposit in a major bank in New York. If it is Euros, it is in Frankfurt or Paris. Yen is in Tokyo.

Banks themselves have been into "offshore" for years. Just look at the annual report of banks like Westpac and ANZ right here in Australia. They have extensive operations in many tax havens! However, the serious money is safe and sound (and generally guaranteed) in their head office. Their "offshore" branches merely facilitate transactions and earn fees.

> If you bank with Citicorp in an "Offshore Financial Centre" country and it all goes horribly wrong in that country, don't worry, your money still exists and being looked after by Citigroup. The quality of the banking organisation itself is all that matters!

Mention to anyone you an offshore account and eyebrows are raised. It's usually followed with a wry smile and a "what are you up to" look. However, I have noticed a change in the last few years with people actually thinking it's the way to go and not being surprised by the whole thing at all.

The Offshore Investment Guide

For many years, big business has regarded offshore banking as being mainstream. More banking transactions by number and volume go through the Cayman Islands and the Bahamas, than go through Switzerland or Germany. Also, more than one third of the world's wealth is held in the top 30 of the world's Offshore Financial Centres (formerly known as Tax Havens). This gives you some idea how "mainstream" the whole "investing and banking offshore" thing has become.

The context of this book is really "International Investing" or Offshore Investing " if you like. This means to take full advantage of the opportunities that would not be available to you locally, you must look at having an offshore banking arrangement. It goes without saying if you are going to have a structure offshore, be it for investing or asset protection, you will need an offshore account to make the whole thing work.

> One of the most important rules to apply when it comes to offshore accounts is use a well-regarded and stable bank. Major international banks would be the preferred option.

Advantages of Offshore Accounts

The main advantages of offshore accounts in most investors' minds are privacy and greater security against seizure, but this is not the whole story.

For instance:

Higher Interest Rates

With the whole world to look at, you may well find banks that offer higher interest rates.

Ability to Diversify into Other Currencies

By banking offshore, you can diversify into other currencies and do your mainstream banking in Euros, US$, UK Sterling, Yen or whatever you like. Or, in many accounts you can even have a mixture of all these currencies so as to really diversify, if you think your own currency is on its way down. Of course, it does bring with it risk and this should be considered.

The "How To" of Global Investment

Lower Fees

You only have to look at your bank statement to realise that you are being skinned alive by your bank with fees. Offshore banks can often be much cheaper.

Better Services and Opportunities

Could there be any dispute on this?

Procedure to Open an Offshore Bank Account

Banks are subject to guidelines and regulations that are designed to ensure that money launderers are unable to utilise banks to hide their assets. Therefore, they require the following information prior to processing an application to open a corporate bank account:

1. A character or Bank reference relating to the beneficial owner(s) and / or controllers of a company addressed to the required bank. The reference should state that the beneficial owner(s) and / or controller(s) has (have) been known to the referee for a period of time and is (are) considered to be trustworthy, respectable and suitable for the purpose of operating a bank account.
2. Certified (by a solicitor) copies of the passport(s) of the beneficial owner(s) and / or controller(s).
3. A description of the company's intended investment and / or trading activities.
4. An indication of what the company's first year's turnover is to be.
5. An initial deposit, to fund the new bank account, commensurate with bank policy.

Note: For personal accounts, only items 1, 2 and 5 would be required.

With changes in all Offshore Financial Centres in relation to money laundering, you will be asked also about the origin of your funds. They need to ensure your money is not as the result of criminal activity. This information is not passed onto government officials, unless of course you are guilty of something.

Internet and Private Banking

Would you like the benefit of a Swiss Bank account as well as pure internet banking?

The Offshore Investment Guide

Well, there is a bank that can give you all that!

First I'll tell you a little about Swiss bank accounts, you know, sort out the fact from the fiction.

The Advantages of Banking with the Swiss

- **Swiss Banks are backed and insured by the Swiss Government.** Unlike any other offshore center, the Swiss Government insures the deposits of all registered banks in Switzerland. Switzerland and its financial institutions are fiercely independent and continuously resistant to outside government threats and attempts at interference. They hold approx. 35% of the world's private assets, or US$2 trillion, are managed and held in Switzerland.
- **Swiss Banks offer the widest selection of available financial services.**
- **Privacy of Swiss Accounts.** Secrecy rules are vigorously enforced throughout the Swiss Banking Industry. This is especially true when it comes to civil matters. Obviously, The Swiss Constitution clearly defines and protects these Secrecy rules. Any Swiss banker revealing information about their clients will be prosecuted under Swiss Law.

  In today's litigation happy society, asset protection and estate planning are the main reasons why people seek Switzerland, as a safe and sound banking centre. People have Swiss Bank Accounts for the privacy and security. No government, tax authority, creditor or agency can ever have information on your account, unless evidence of serious crime can be produced. Bank secrecy can only be removed by a Federal Judge and for criminal reasons (money laundering, serious crime, arms and drugs sales) but never for tax avoidance or asset protection or lawsuit inquiries.
- **Safety in Swiss Francs.** The Swiss National Bank has one of the highest reserves of Gold bullion to back up its currency. Over the last few decades the Swiss franc has held its value better than any other currency in the world. At market prices, actual gold reserves significantly exceed currency in circulation. Switzerland has the fourth largest gold holding in the world. But reserves do not consist only of gold. Non-gold reserves are almost five times as high as gold reserves.
- **Switzerland itself is safe.** Inflation in Switzerland consistently remains low. Switzerland is the only country that has never imposed exchange controls. Switzerland has not been involved in

The "How To" of Global Investment

war this century and this prevents destruction by remaining neutral, while having an active army. Switzerland's national referendum system ensures that its people have a vote and the country will remain a strong, thriving democracy. Switzerland has a low terrorist risk due to its balanced, neutral foreign policy. The nation can also protect 98% of its population in shelters, which protects them from nuclear, biological and chemical attack. This also reduces the risk of terrorist threats.

- **Swiss bankers are fluent in most major languages**
- **Swiss bank accounts allow holding foreign currencies.** Swiss francs, Euros, UK pounds, US$, Yen, Australian and Canadian dollars.

> *In Switzerland..... tax authorities cannot lift bank secrecy for tax assessment or tax evasion matters –*
> Australian Taxation Office February 2004

Now, To The Bank........

Swissquote Bank has already acquired considerable experience and a large client base through their Swissquote Trade site (www.swissquote.com), which has operated online brokerage services on the Swissquote financial portal since November 1999. It has nearly 10,000 customers and a market share of 15%. It is ranked third on the Swiss market behind the two big banks, UBS and Credit Suisse.

The leading banks in Switzerland, UBS and Credit Suisse, have developed a major online presence and also offer similar services, but Swissquote Bank is the first Swiss bank to function only online without any supporting bricks-and-mortar branches.

Their head office is located in Gland, which is on the banks of the Lake of Geneva.

Swissquote Bank was the brainchild of two former graduates of the leading polytechnic in Western Switzerland (EPFL), which is noted for its strong encouragement of start-ups. Marc Bürki and Paolo Buzzi share the CEO responsibilities. They created the company in 1997 after several years of active involvement in the development of innovative web based information services. Swissquote specialises in the diffusion, in real-time, of financial information via the Internet, as well as in several leading Swiss daily newspapers. It is one of Switzerland's most visited

The Offshore Investment Guide

financial information sites, with an average of 3.2 million page views every working day.

Features of the Bank Swissquote:
- It is the only bank in Switzerland that offers online banking and investing, to almost all global citizens.
- Funds available, including a bond fund that holds government securities, has paid 6+% annually over the past 5 years.
- A personal banker is assigned to your banking relationship, that is fluent in English, French and German.
- Motivated staff who are eager to assist you in achieving your financial goals.
- Payment can be made abroad, to any country, in any desired currency. You can choose between, wire transfer or a cheque or use your ATM card.
- 24 Hour World-wide access to your funds. ATM and VISA available.
- Transfer money into your bank account anytime, anywhere, no limits
- Deposit cheques in any currency
- Wire Money around the world
- They make offshore bank account setup easy
- Just a copy of your passport or ID required.
- 24/7 online real-time banking system
- Transfer to and from any bank in the world

Contact them at:

http://bank.swissquote.ch
or
http://www.swissquote.ch

Offshore Banking – An Australian Perspective

Generally speaking, Australia is not considered an advantageous location for those interested in tax minimisation, and has a comprehensive taxation system in place. Residency is assumed if an individual has his or her permanent home there, if it is their normal place of residence, if they have close

> **Australia**
>
> There are no exchange controls and you can move your money into and out of the country at will. Offshore banking is permitted and legal

The "How To" of Global Investment

economic ties, or they've been in Australia either continuously or intermittently for more than 183 days in any tax year. Residents are taxed on their world-wide income, simple as that. Keep in mind there is a big difference between "residency" and citizenship.

There are no exchange controls and you can move your money into and out of the country at will. Offshore banking is permitted and legal.

There are a considerable number of tax treaties, and tax paid on foreign income is normally allowed as a credit against Australian tax. However, foreign 'passive' income (i.e. dividends, interest, royalties etc) is treated as a separate class of income, and tax credits are segregated according to class. Depending on individual circumstances, it may therefore be best for an Australian tax-resident to make sure that any money placed on deposit abroad is not taxed at origin unless they are sure a foreign tax credit is allowed.

Popular Offshore Banking destinations for Australians

Vanuatu

There are more than 100 banks established in Vanuatu, making it the leading offshore banking centre in this part of the world. The great majority of these banks are 'exempted', i.e. they have limited banking licenses and do not offer banking services domestically.

Banking in Vanuatu is regulated by the Reserve Bank of Vanuatu. The licensing of banks is carried out by the Financial Services Commission. Exempted banks are not subject to the Banking Act's prudential rules, but the Financial Services Commission applies fairly stringent criteria to applicants for exempted bank status.

Exempted banks offer deposit and other asset management services, but do not offer cheque accounts - for that, one must go to a 'local' bank with a full banking licence. A few international banks have such licenses, including several major Australian banks, such as Westpac and ANZ.

There are no taxes in Vanuatu on profits, dividends or income for either resident or non-resident individuals.

Hong Kong

Hong Kong is one of the foremost international banking centres in the world, with 65 of the largest banks having established a presence there. There is a 3 tier system of banking institutions in place: licensed banks; restricted licensed banks; and deposit taking companies. Hong Kong

The Offshore Investment Guide

has no central bank as such, but the Hong Kong Monetary Authority does assume many of the responsibilities typically assigned to a central bank, including ensuring the safety and soundness of the banking system and the stability of the currency. Hong Kong adheres to the Basel principles for bank supervision.

Under the Sino-British Joint Declaration on the Future of Hong Kong, Chinese authorities were committed to enact the Basic Law of the Hong Kong Special Administrative Region. The Basic Law is the legal basis for the "One Country, Two Systems" guarantee and provides for the continuance of Hong Kong's system of common law and free market economic system after 1 July 1997.

The Law stipulates that the Hong Kong dollar will remain freely convertible; that markets for foreign exchange, securities, futures, and other financial products will remain open; and that no controls will be placed on the flow of capital into or out of Hong Kong.

Although it is considered by some to be an offshore jurisdiction, Hong Kong is better described as a low tax area, which levies tax according to the territorial principle. Personal income tax is known as Salaries Tax, and individuals, whether resident or not, are taxed only on income "arising in or derived from a Hong Kong employment" Therefore, non-employment source income such as bank interest and share dividends is not taxable in the territory either for residents or non-residents.

Hong Kong banks evidently offer a world-class array of financial services of all types. Deposits can be made in many different currencies, but as might be expected deposit rates may not be the most attractive in widely-used local or global currencies.

Offshore Banking – A British Perspective

The UK is not a very advantageous location for those interested in tax limitation, although it does compare favourably with most EU countries, other than Ireland and Luxembourg. If you are resident in the UK (that is if you live there for more than 182 days per tax year, have spent more than 91 days there per tax year over 4 years, or make prolonged and habitual visits to the country), you are liable to pay income tax.

Non-residence is assumed when you have spent 1 complete tax year overseas, during which your return visits total less than 92 days (excluding days of travel). As a non-resident, you are liable to tax on

The "How To" of Global Investment

certain types of UK source income and gains. For example: UK property; any trade or profession, which has a UK based branch; and employment duties performed in the UK. You are not, however, liable to tax on the interest from certain government securities, or interest from UK situated banks and building society deposits.

Popular Offshore Banking Destinations for the British

The Isle of Man

The Isle of Man, with approximately 75 banking operations established, is a prime location for UK expatriates and foreign nationals wishing to bank offshore. The industry on the island, is dominated by branches or subsidiaries of the main UK clearing banks, although there are also some foreign banks. Banking services provided range from deposit taking to establishing and administering trusts, managing the underlying companies and assets held by those trusts, and investment management. Banks on the Isle of Man are supervised by the Financial Services Commission (FSC).

The Banking Act recognises the contractual duty of a banker to keep the affairs of his customer confidential and the customers' entitlement to confidentiality, other than where disclosure is required to assist criminal proceedings or to enable the FSC to discharge its statutory functions.

All banking licence holders are required to participate in the Depositors Compensation Scheme. The FSC is the Scheme Manager. Deposits are protected up to 75% of the first £20,000 per depositor (or foreign currency equivalent).

A number of Manx banks offer a range of current and deposit accounts designed especially for non-residents and expatriates. There are no rules to prevent UK nationals from opening an account on the Isle of Man, whether UK resident or not. Accounts are available in a number of currencies, and interest rates are comparable with or slightly above those offered onshore. There are also several banks offering Internet on-line banking services from the Isle of Man

By concession, deposit interest from Manx banks payable to non-residents (of Man) is exempt from income tax. Isle of Man residents pay 20% income tax.

Guernsey in The Channel Islands

There are over 70 banking establishments on Guernsey, all of which are subsidiaries or branches of foreign banks, and are regulated by the Financial Services Commission (FSC). Following from the boom period

The Offshore Investment Guide

of the 1980's, Guernsey's deposit base has continued to grow, and has become more international. The FSC is extremely careful to exclude doubtful operations, and has capital adequacy rules, which are stiffer than the Basel requirements.

A number of Guernsey banks offer a range of current and deposit accounts designed especially for non-residents and expatriates. There are no rules to prevent UK nationals from opening an account in Guernsey, whether UK resident or not. Accounts are available in a number of currencies, and interest rates are comparable with or slightly above those offered onshore.

By concession, deposit interest from Guernsey banks payable to non-residents (of Guernsey) is exempt from income tax. Guernsey residents pay 20% income tax.

Jersey in The Channel Islands

Jersey's financial and advisory infrastructure is very well developed, with over 80 banks comprised mainly of subsidiaries or branches of the top US and UK banks, with Switzerland, Canada, Germany and many other countries also represented. Banks are regulated by the Financial Services Commission, and capital adequacy rules are tighter than those under the Basel Convention.

Many Jersey banks offer a range of current and deposit accounts designed especially for non-residents and expatriates. There are no rules to prevent UK nationals from opening an account in Jersey, whether UK resident or not. Accounts are available in a number of currencies, and interest rates are comparable with those offered onshore.

By concession, deposit interest from Jersey banks payable to non-residents (of Jersey) is exempt from income tax. Jersey residents pay 20% income tax.

Gibraltar

The banking sector of Gibraltar is very well established, with offshore banking especially advantageous in this jurisdiction due to its favourable tax regime, lack of exchange controls, political stability, good communications network, and the internet banking services offered by many banks. There are approximately thirty banks established in Gibraltar, comprising mainly branches of the top UK, US, and European banks. The Commissioner of Banking regulates banking in Gibraltar under The Banking Ordinance 1992; the supervisory regime follows EU and Basel Committee guidelines.

The "How To" of Global Investment

A deposit protection policy is being brought into effect by the Gibraltar Deposit Guarantee Board in line with EU directives in this area The amount of compensation payable to any claimant is the lesser of 90% of the total amount of all the claimant's qualifying deposits or £18,000 (or the sterling equivalent of ECU20,000 if it is greater than £18,000).

Much of the banking activity in Gibraltar is directed to asset management for high-net-worth individuals, not least because Gibraltar has tried hard to attract such people, with special tax regimes. Although Gibraltar has no double tax treaties, there are arrangements with the UK to limit double taxation of income.

Some Gibraltar banks offer a range of current and deposit accounts designed especially for non-residents and expatriates. There are no rules to prevent UK nationals from opening an account in Gibraltar, whether UK resident or not. Accounts are available in a number of currencies, and interest rates are comparable with those offered onshore.

By concession, deposit interest from Gibraltar banks payable to non-residents (of Gibraltar) is exempt from income tax. Gibraltar residents would pay income tax of up to 35%, however. An individual is considered resident in Gibraltar if he has accommodation there and sets foot on the territory during the tax year.

Ireland

The Irish banking sector has grown extremely rapidly over the last few years, with the IFSC (International Financial Services Centre) providing a favourable environment for offshore banking. Ireland offers foreign currency services, global money management, facilities for dealing and trading in securities dominated by foreign currency, and a host of other services. The Central Bank of Ireland regulates the banking industry and ensures that banking operations are consistent with the safety of depositors' funds, prudent banking practices and fair trading in banking.

Banks in the IFSC don't have to deduct withholding tax on interest payments made to non-residents. In any event, Ireland has signed a double tax treaty with the United Kingdom, which ensures that no tax is withheld on interest paid to the UK. There would be withholding tax (currently 24%) on interest paid to residents.

As in many countries, residence is consequent on presence in Ireland for more than half of a tax year, or for 280 days in two consecutive years. A non-resident individual pays income tax only on Irish-sourced income, and is liable to capital gains tax only on gains arising in Ireland

The Offshore Investment Guide

or remitted to Ireland, unless he is domiciled in Ireland in which case he is liable on all capital gains.

Offshore Banking – An American Perspective

Because the US taxes its citizens on the basis of their nationality and not on the basis of their residence, the concept of 'offshore' is not very useful to a US national from a residence point of view. There is an income tax concession on $76,000 of foreign earned income available during non-residence, but beyond that the tax position of an individual US citizen is

> **USA**
> There is an income tax concession on US$76,000 of foreign earned income available during non-residence

about the same whether they are in or out of the US. The tax position of a 'non-resident alien' is fairly favourable, but the rules determining residence are extensive, and difficult to escape. For taxation purposes, you are considered US resident if you meet either the Green card or substantial presence criterion. Non-resident aliens pay tax on US-source income, but are not liable to tax on capital gains or bank and portfolio interest. Dividends, and other types of interest are charged 30% withholding tax.

Non-resident US citizens must be aware that tax paid in another jurisdiction may not be reclaimable against US tax, if there is no double tax treaty - often the case with offshore jurisdictions.

Residents are liable for tax on their world-wide income, and any US citizen deemed to have expatriated for tax reasons is also liable for 10 years after their departure.

US expatriates, unless they have formally broken their bond with the US, can gain no financial advantage from offshore banking; however, there may be other reasons for wishing to use an offshore bank account, such as asset protection.

Popular Offshore Banking Destination for Americans
Bermuda

The Bermuda government made an early decision to exclude foreign banks, and as a result there are only 3 Bermudan banks, supervised by the Bermuda Monetary Authority. These offer a wide range of banking

The "How To" of Global Investment

services, however, and have expanded throughout the world, with subsidiaries in the major financial centres.

Bermuda laws do not give any protection to Bermuda depositors or checking account users or savers.

> When you think about it, if the US and British banks provide the bulk of banking services to Offshore Investors, and therefore make the profits, and then pay those profits to shareholders in predominately their home countries, and pay tax to their home government, how logical is it for the US and British governments to close down these operations totally?..... The answer is...
>
> It isn't and they won't, not totally.

A number of foreign controlled financial advisories and securities firms have been established, and can provide financial services such as electronic brokerage, international dealing and trading, and securities issuance and custody (they cannot, however take deposits).

Basic personal banking services are provided exclusively by the two main local banks. This is a phenomenon, which is something of an exception for an OFC. In most OFC's, it is the large British and US banks that provide the bulk of banking services.

Just let me digress here for a minute also. When you think about it, if the US and British banks provide all the banking services to Offshore Investors, and therefore make the profits, and then pay those profits to shareholders in predominately their home countries, and pay tax to their home government, how logical is it for the US and British governments to close down these operations totally?..... The answer is... it isn't and they won't, not totally.

There is no income tax, capital gains tax, purchase or sales tax in Bermuda. (There are taxes on property and customs duties, which can be significant for immigrants.)

US citizens can therefore make tax-free deposits in Bermuda; the problem is that rates are not likely to be competitive with those obtainable elsewhere. This is evidently a result of the lack of banking competition on the island, but also because of the very high fees charged to the banks by the Government. These, together with employment taxes levied on the labour-intensive banks ensure high cost ratios and expensive services.

101

The Offshore Investment Guide

The Bahamas

The Bahamas is one of the world's top ten international banking centers, with 400 licensed banks from more than 30 countries, and a total asset base around $200bn. Capital ratios average over 10%. The Central Bank of the Bahamas applies stiff criteria to incoming banks in order to exclude money laundering and criminal activity. In response to international pressure in 2001, the financial supervisory regime in the Bahamas has been extensively renovated, and previously high standards of banking privacy have been to some extent undermined in the process.

Private banking is a major component of the Bahamian banking industry, with asset protection rather than tax avoidance as such, being the driving force. The stability of the Bahamas alongside stringent banking secrecy and its sophisticated investment environment are very attractive to wealthy individuals, particularly those from the US, where the Bahamas have a very good reputation

Exchange controls in the Bahamas apply only to the Bahamian dollar, and there are no capital or exchange controls for non-residents.

The majority of Bahamian taxes are levied in relation to events rather than residential status. Non-residents are liable for taxes on any developed or undeveloped real estate they may own on the islands, and customs duties are quite high on the majority of imported goods. However, there is no income tax, capital gains tax, purchase or sales tax, VAT or capital transfer tax, and because direct taxes are not levied, there is no need for double taxation treaties between the Bahamas and other countries.

> United States citizens pay taxes on their worldwide income regardless of where they live…. They are taxed on their citizenship, residency like Australians and Brits…… Paradoxically, the US is a safe haven for 90% of the world's investors and foreign banks….. To encourage investment into their markets, no capital gains taxes are due on foreigners who play the US market……
> Interestingly, if you were an expat Australian or Brit, and were actually living in a low tax haven, like Hong Kong, you could speculate and trade the US market and pay virtually no tax on your gains…… 100% legally! No a bad thought…. Spend 5 years overseas, make your money and come back and retire.

The "How To" of Global Investment

US citizens are therefore able to bank tax-free in the Bahamas, although now that the IRS's 'Qualified Intermediary' regime is in force (from January 1 2001), they will be able to avoid deduction of US withholding tax in the Bahamas, only if they have presented adequate tax documentation to the bank concerned.

Deposits can be made in a number of major currencies in the Bahamas, but the best interest rates are likely to be offered in the US dollar, which has a dominant position in the country's financial structure.

Panama

Due to a combination of factors, including the absence of exchange controls, liberal banking legislation, and strict secrecy provisions, Panama has developed as a major financial centre for Latin America and the Caribbean, with more than 100 licensed banks from more than 20 countries in 1997. Banking is governed by the Banking Law (1970), and the National Banking Commission grants banking licences and fulfils some of the responsibilities of a central bank. The Commission is selective in granting banking licenses, and looks for an established history and good reputation, preferring branches to subsidiaries due to the more direct parental control structure.

Residence is assumed if an individual is present in Panama for more than 180 days in any tax year, but for taxation purposes, no distinction is made between residents and non-residents. Taxation is levied on a territorial basis, and only income or gains derived through business carried on in Panama itself is liable for income tax. As Panama does not tax foreign source income, it has no double tax treaties with any other countries. Interest on deposits with Panamanian banks is exempt from taxation whatever the source of the cash.

US citizens are therefore able to bank tax-free in Panama, although now that the IRS's new 'Qualified Intermediary' regime is in force (from January 1 2001), they are able to avoid deduction of US withholding tax in Panama, only if they have presented adequate tax documentation to the bank concerned.

Deposits can be made in a number of major currencies in Panama, but the best interest rates are likely to be offered in the US dollar, which has a dominant position in the country's financial structure.

The Offshore Investment Guide

If you would like to know much more on Offshore Banking, privacy and secrecy, tricks of the trade, lists of banks, advantages and disadvantages of various banking centres, then I suggest you obtain a copy of my book, Invisible Banking.

International Banks Know "The System"

If a large German bank were to make a billion Euro loan to Chrysler Benz to expand its Mexican factory, it would have to pay a substantial amount of tax on all the interest received. Plus there would be national income taxes due on the many other charges (appraisals, environmental impact reports) tacked on by the bank, in the course of making a loan. By booking the loan through their branch office in a low tax or no tax jurisdiction like say, Panama, the bank escapes all or most taxes. They can save enough tax money on one single deal to build a skyscraper in Panama. Instead of bringing profits home, where they are taxed, banks do plough tax haven profits back into expensive office buildings and other investments in the offshore centre. That's why a place like Panama City looks like Manhattan.

Why do most governments allow banks to escape taxes by booking business and profits in offshore tax haven branches? Simple, because every country wants strong banks. If all the other banks could book offshore business tax-free and banks of say the USA always had 50% of every profit taxed away; they would become smaller and non-competitive. Another obvious reason is that banks and insurance companies have good lobbyists. Banks with offshore branches make a lot of donations to be sure the government understands and is sympathetic to their point of view.

The "How To" of Global Investment

How Offshore Works & Understanding Your Needs

As we have already discussed, a growing number of business and professional people are considering offshore options. Most appear to be focused on the fundamental issues of:
- Privacy
- Asset Protection
- Investment
- Estate Planning
- Tax Benefits

Over the years, most people have been focused on the last one, tax benefits. This is a serious mistake, particularly these days. If the only reason one has for going offshore is tax avoidance, I recommend strongly that one seek the assistance of a qualified tax advisor and explore the myriad of opportunities available for onshore tax deferral or minimisation first.

The benefits for "going offshore" are still great even if one were to eliminate "tax benefits" altogether. Now, I'm not saying that tax benefits don't exist, they do, but don't make that your "only reason". With changes to legislation worldwide and the clampdown on money laundering, many tax evaders may be caught in the net and find themselves with serious problems.

The Australian Tax Office, Revenue Canada and the IRS in the USA all continue to take the position, that when the primary reason an offshore option is invoked is tax deferral or avoidance, this motivation alone, once articulated, is and of itself sufficient grounds to deny any tax benefit. It is important therefore that anyone considering an offshore business opportunity do so for reasons other than tax issues alone. Yes,

The Offshore Investment Guide

the tax issue may be "a" reason for going offshore but it should not be the only or principal reason.

There are a number of very important reasons for one to consider expanding their business activities offshore. These are in addition to the truly significant benefits of privacy and asset protection, and tax benefits.

Motivating factors may include:
- An offshore company can invest in global securities including top performing mutual funds not available to Australian or U.S. citizens.
- Privacy is often integral to risk planning. Offshore clients typically seek confidentiality in their affairs to protect business strategies.
- Offshore jurisdictions are generally less business invasive allowing for aggressive and unrestrained enterprise with lower overheads.
- An offshore corporation may be used to file first position liens against assets and property, thereby closing the "apparent" window of vulnerability to predatory litigation and stop frivolous litigation before it commences.
- By titling property into an offshore company, you can transfer real estate, cars, boats, and other property more easily by selling or transferring the shares or ownership of the company instead of re-titling the property when sold.
- An offshore company may be used to segregate high-risk investments from other more secure holdings such as investment real estate.
- Offshore legal structures are widely recognised as one of the best ways for segregating assets and achieving privacy from potential litigation.
- An offshore structure can be used as an effective prenuptial agreement.
- Protecting your retirement "Nestegg" from possible bankruptcy.
- Estate planning: Provide for the transfer of assets for the next generation in an efficient and discreet fashion. Using an offshore trust would be the best way to achieve this.
- An offshore company, in conjunction with nominee directors and officers, can allow you to conduct business transactions for your benefit while you remain anonymous.
- By transferring assets out of harm's way, different types of insurance costs may be substantially reduced.
- An offshore company may be used as a holding vehicle for properties with potential litigation problems.

The "How To" of Global Investment

- When used in conjunction with corporate debit or credit cards, an offshore corporation can maintain a degree of financial confidentiality with your transactions.
- Used in conjunction with a carefully structured plan, tax may sometimes be legally delayed or minimised. Several countries such as Australia, Canada and the U.S. have enacted anti-avoidance legislation designed to reduce the use of tax haven countries for strictly tax avoidance reasons. Tax haven countries are now generally referred to as Offshore Financial Centers, ("OFCs") and it's interesting to note that their very existence began as an effect of UK and American efforts, to reduce aid to specific developing nations. Instead of providing foreign aid, legislation was passed to grant incentives for multinational corporations to invest in target offshore jurisdictions. Hasn't that all backfired on them? Now, they are doing their best to reduce these countries' economic viability by reducing the opportunities available to investors.

You must remember, the simple act of setting up an offshore corporation does not automatically, reduce tax liability for the individual. This is the way it was 20 years ago, but not now.

Notwithstanding the above, OFCs have become a critical part of the tax planning strategies of individuals and corporations doing business worldwide. Medium to high net worth individuals are increasingly using offshore entities (companies and trusts, or a combination of both) in order to take advantage of investment opportunities unavailable to them in their home country.

The Australian Securities and Investments Commission (ASIC), and the Securities & Exchange Commissions (SEC) in both Canada and the US, for example, require investment companies to provide an exhaustive and extremely expensive prospectus before an investment may be offered to their citizens and residents.

Many of the top performing offshore funds find the filing process unnecessarily demanding and uneconomical in high tax countries. Instead these funds prefer to invest the money they have saved, thereby improving overall return. The result is greater returns and less legal hassles.

> Many of the 6,000 "offshore funds" available throughout the world today are essentially unavailable to Australian, UK and US citizens.

Other funds that are "onshore" based tend to bypass countries like Australia, reducing our opportunity to invest in the "best

The Offshore Investment Guide

of the best". Simply, as we are insignificant sized markets.

Many of the 6,000 "offshore funds" available throughout the world today are essentially unavailable to Australian, UK and US citizens. It's interesting to note that all these funds are based in traditional "tax haven" countries. For example: 55% are in Luxembourg, 13% in Guernsey & Jersey, 9% in the Isle of Man, 5% are in the Cayman Islands, 4% in Bermuda, 2% in the British Virgin Islands, and the rest are scattered throughout the globe.

Many are British Commonwealth island jurisdictions, which does make you wonder about the UK's efforts to reduce their prominence. Ultimately, it's the Crown that profits from these "Offshore Financial Centres". However, the bottom line is an "offshore company or trust" can easily invest in any of these funds or investments available worldwide. These passive investments must be disclosed in most countries and capital gains taxes paid in most cases.

The decision to utilise an offshore trust or company to form and operate an offshore setup is one that should be carefully considered. If tax avoidance is the primary motivation, one should expect a number of obstacles that must be dealt with prior to taking action. However, if your goal is to access new markets, take advantage of business and investment opportunities unavailable at home, and protect your assets from frivolous and predatory litigation, use of an offshore corporation could provide you with substantial future benefits.

The Offshore Structures – How they Work

There are basically two offshore structures the offshore investor can use, the company and the trust. Now, for some of you, you may not have read my other books on offshore investment, such as The Invisible World, so I should give a you a quick rundown on them, and to those who have been through all this before, this may help as a bit of revision.

The Offshore Company

The Offshore Company is often referred to as an IBC or International Business Company. There is very little difference between the IBC and a normal local company. They operate pretty much the same way. It is just that the offshore company is, well, ... offshore.

The "How To" of Global Investment

One other difference between the onshore and offshore company, apart from the geographic issue, is that an IBC is only allowed to trade *outside* its own country. It can't setup "shop" in its own country or hold property there, but it can bank there. However, it is ideal for the offshore investor.

So, what can an Offshore Company be used for?

- **Trading Company**

An importing or exporting company might establish itself in an offshore area. The offshore company would take orders directly from the customer, but have the goods delivered directly to that customer from the manufacturer or place of purchase. The profits arising out of the difference between purchase price and sales price would then be accumulated in either a tax free or low tax area. With such trading companies, it is important to choose an offshore area, which has good communications, as you can imagine. Dubai has become a very popular country for this purpose. An emerging area of offshore trading is E-Commerce.

- **Investment Company**

An offshore investment company is ideal, as it gives you access to many offshore investment opportunities, not normally available to you.

- **Holding Company**

This company could hold the shares of other offshore or onshore companies in a much larger structure.

- **Probate and Privacy**

A high net worth person with properties or other assets in a number of countries, may wish to hold these through a personal holding company so that upon his death, probate (where it applies) would be applied for in the country in which his company was incorporated, rather than in each of the countries in which he might hold assets. This saves legal fees and avoids publicity. Again, not everybody wishes to advertise wealth and an individual may wish to hold property through an offshore entity simply because of the privacy, which the offshore arrangement gives.

- **Property Owning**

There are often great advantages in using an offshore property holding company for the purpose of holding an overseas property. Advantages of offshore property ownership include:
   1. Avoidance of inheritance tax in, for instance the UK
   2. Ease of sale, which is achieved by transferring the shares in the company rather than transferring the property owned by the company

The Offshore Investment Guide

3. Reduction of property purchase costs to the onward purchasers.

- **Professional Services**

Individuals who receive substantial fees in respect of their professional services, in capacities such as designers, consultants, authors or entertainers, may assign or contract with an offshore company, the right to receive those fees. There can be tax benefits derived, depending on residency status etc.

- **Shipping Companies**

The use of offshore shipping companies can eliminate direct or indirect taxation on shipping. Shipping companies may own or charter ships, the profits from which activities can be accumulated tax-free. Tax and legal requirements generally dictate that the offshore company owning a ship should be incorporated in the jurisdiction whose flag the ship flies. Historically, havens for these purposes have been Panama and Liberia.

- **Patent, Copyright and Royalty Companies**

An offshore company can purchase or be assigned the right to use a copyright, patent, trademark or know-how by its original holders with a power to sublicence. Upon acquisition of the intellectual property rights, the offshore company can then enter into agreement with licensees around the world, who would be able to exploit the intellectual property rights in various countries.

- **Trustee Company**

Very useful when putting together an offshore structure, particularly in regard to asset protection. The IBC becomes the trustee and the trust holds all the assets or investments.

Consider the following factors carefully:

If you are looking to establish an offshore company, it needs to be both safe and secure.

Also look into:
- Compliance requirements
- Permitted company names and suffixes to denote limited liability
- Minimum capital requirements
- Requirements to hold directors and/or shareholder meetings
- Filing obligations and procedures
- Requirement (if any) for the audit of accounting records
- Number of shareholders and directors
- Disclosure requirements

The "How To" of Global Investment

Whilst there is a lot more to be considered in this area, like jurisdictions, laws, tax regulations, confidentiality, structures etc, these are all covered in my book The Invisible World.

Establishing the Offshore Company
Before incorporation, the appropriate registrar must approve the company name. In all jurisdictions, certain words such as international, bank, trust, insurance and holdings might be, and usually are, subject to minimum capital requirements, licensing or other local regulations. A shelf company is a common technique to begin trading immediately.

Appointing Shareholders
Most jurisdictions require a minimum of one or more shareholders, who are the legal owners, but not necessarily the beneficial owners. Individuals, companies or trustees can all be shareholders. A shareholder's details are submitted to the registrar in jurisdictions that require an annual return. Reputable advisory companies offer services that include nominee shareholders, who can act on behalf of the client.

Appointing Directors and Company Secretary
Most jurisdictions require a minimum of one or more director, who must be natural persons, but many jurisdictions permit corporate directors. These are companies that act as directors of other companies for privacy purposes. Company directors control day-to-day affairs and the company secretary prepares and files statutory accounts and the annual return.

Issue of Authorised Share Capital
The capital available for issue to shareholders is known as Authorised Share Capital. Usually, it can be designated in any currency. It may be issued in part or full, or for non-monetary consideration. Companies are generally allowed to modify the share capital, if all shareholders agree.

Choosing a Registered Office Address
In most jurisdictions of incorporation, an offshore company must have a registered office sited there. This is the company's legal address and where its statutory records are maintained. Business can be conducted from this office or from another location or country. Normally, this office is operated by your incorporation agent, for a fee, of course.

Offshore Banking Accounts
An incorporation agent can help choose an offshore bank that is:
- Familiar with offshore and international business
- Has a global investment and business perspective
- Is tax-efficient
- Guarantees confidentiality

The Offshore Investment Guide

- Has a lack of foreign exchange controls
- Has access to special investment opportunities

For a typical offshore company, the procedure will be:
- Your agent will request certain information in accordance with due diligence procedure.
- Incorporation of the company on your behalf, using your chosen name, or provision of a ready-made 'shelf' company.
- Usually, one or two senior personnel of your agent are appointed as directors of the company.
- A company secretary to maintain the statutory records and to ensure compliance with statutory requirements is also usually appointed by the agent.
- Your agent can also provide nominee shareholders to hold the shares on your behalf.
- Your agent can often arrange to open an offshore bank account for you.
- Provision of registered office facilities is offered by your agent.
- Bank signatories are often also provided if you require them.
- Finally, an agreement is executed between the agent and you concerning the operation of the company and the obligations of both parties.

Now, this is typical and applies to Australian, UK and US situations. However, there are many variations on this theme to suit individual situations. There are also some very intricate tax laws to negotiate as well as some tricks to ensure that your assets are 100% safe. This is all discussed and disclosed in The Invisible World.

An offshore company will cost around AUD$2,000+ depending on what requirements you have.

The Offshore Trust

A trust is an entity by which a person hands ownership and control of his or her assets to a trusted third party (the "Trustee") to operate for the benefit of "Beneficiaries". This gives the person who "settles" the trust, known as the "Settlor" the ability to divest himself of ownership of his assets, with several resulting benefits.

The Settlor will choose trustees he can rely upon completely, to look after his or her assets and carry out their wishes for the administration and eventual distribution of the assets.

The document setting out the structure of the trust is called the Trust Deed and a lot of care has to be taken in drafting this, taking into

The "How To" of Global Investment

account the person's situation, particularly regarding tax, and the nature of the assets to be transferred to the trust. Specific beneficiaries should be named in the Trust Deed, but these people don't have to necessarily exist. For example: your unborn grandchildren.

The Trustees administer the trust at their discretion, but a "Letter of Wishes" is often drawn up by the Settlor, setting out how he would like the trust to be run. In practice, the Trustees will operate in accordance with the Letter of Wishes but are not necessarily legally bound to do so. However, as I discussed before, when talking about Asset Protection, the best situation to have, is an offshore company as the trustee and you as the director of the "trustee company". This could of course change, depending on what you are trying to achieve with all of this. We will get to some more specific examples a little later on.

Though there are several types of trust structure, the most common established are discretionary trusts, those where the Trustees have full discretion in the administration and disposal of the assets, for the benefit of the beneficiaries.

The Trustee must operate in the best interests of the Beneficiaries, and may break the law if they fail to exercise a sufficient level of care. They must obey the directions in the Trust Deed and must account for all transactions. They are entitled to make reasonable charges, but are not permitted to derive any advantage from the Trust themselves. Their actions are strictly controlled by law.

What are the advantages of a trust?

- **Continuity:**
Assets in a bank account may be lost on the death of the account holder. If the account is held by a Trust, continuity beyond death is assured and it will not be necessary to prove ownership. The use of a corporate trustee prevents problems should an individual trustee die.
- **Asset Protection:**
The Settlor, having handed over his assets to the Trustees, no longer owns these assets so they cannot be seized in cases of insolvency, marital proceedings or professional negligence. If however, the Trust was set up intentionally to avoid a known current or future liability it may be set aside by the courts, as we discussed earlier in the book.
- **Inheritance Planning:**
The assets of the trust are not included in the Settlor's will, as they are not legally his property. This gives the opportunity to make

The Offshore Investment Guide

specific transfers of assets to Beneficiaries outside the rules applied in some countries, as to who may inherit.
- **Flexibility:**
It is possible to make specific provisions in the event of death as to children's education and income, life income for the widow, establishment of contingency funds, etc.

A trust prevents the division of assets amongst heirs at the time of death so that the fund can be protected and accumulated. Assets may be preserved for later generations. A trust may also prevent the forced sale of a family business or other assets. In this way, a trust can maintain a family legacy for future generations.

Who are you? What is your Scenario?

Everybody has different situations to deal with but often they come down to three common scenarios, and they are:
- Resident Planning to go Offshore
- Resident Planning to stay at home
- Businessperson or Executive Working Offshore

I thought it would be helpful just to clarify these situations further, even though they were discussed in the International Tax Planning and Legalities Chapter. I've also then presented the scenarios of Australians, Americans and British seeing so many of my books are now entering these markets.

Understanding the regulations related to tax and residency is fundamental in the planning of an offshore structure, so I hope you don't think I'm spending too much time on it.

The Situation for Australians

Australian Resident Planning to go Offshore

There are some differences between permanent and temporary non-residence.

Temporary non-residence

If a resident goes overseas to work but his term of employment overseas is less than 2 years and he intends returning to Australia then he will not be taxed as non-resident, although his employment earnings as such, will be exempt from Australian tax.

The "How To" of Global Investment

An individual spending a limited period overseas (eg a diplomat or a business executive) will probably be in a favourable income tax situation during non-residence. However, the FIF legislation punishes ownership of foreign assets on return to Australia by taxing their accumulated gains, so there is not much point in trying to acquire such assets during a period of non-residence unless a very long absence is in view. After taxation on return home, offshore assets acquired during non-residence will have the same status as those acquired during residence, so there is no extra advantage to be gained from offshore investment due to non-residence as such.

Expatriate Australians can however invest in Australian share assets and will not be subject to Australian capital gains tax on realised gains during non-residence providing that the shares have been held for 5 years and that they do not amount to more than a 10% holding in the company concerned. They can also invest in shares, which pay fully franked dividends and not be subject to further Australian tax. Another advantage of investment into Australian shares is that there will be no administrative or financial problems on return home.

One of the most interesting investment opportunities open to temporarily expatriate Australians may be an Employer Sponsored Foreign Superannuation Fund. If such a fund complies with certain conditions, it benefits from considerable investment and tax advantages. The key conditions include the following:

- The funds must be established and/or maintained by an employer and must be genuinely for retirement provision;
- It must be established and have residency outside Australia;
- It must not benefit from concessional tax treatment in Australia;
- It must not invest in Australia

An approved fund may invest funds in offshore capital markets. While the expatriate is non-resident, participation in such a fund will not be subject to tax in Australia under FIF, CGT, FLP, or any other rules. Importantly, when returning to Australia, the expatriate may bring all or any part of their accumulated entitlement into Australia, within 6 months, completely tax-free. This can then be rolled over into a complying fund or approved deposit fund in Australia, with the accompanying tax benefits.

Any accrued benefits which are not brought back into Australia within 6 months of the expatriate's return will be subject to tax in Australia, but only on the difference between the benefits the expatriate finally receives and the value of the accrued entitlement on the day that the expatriate returns to Australia. In some cases, this could give rise to significant tax benefits.

The Offshore Investment Guide

Permanent non-residence

Due to the FIF and other sets of Australian tax rules, there are relatively few types of offshore investment available to Australian residents, which can maintain deferral of tax until after departure.

Once departure has taken place, the situation is different, and if the decision not to return to residence is a firm one, the Australian expatriate is reasonably free to invest wherever he can get the best returns.

Once a definite decision to move offshore has been made, careful thought should also be given to existing Australian capital assets, including pension assets. Will it be possible to move them offshore without incurring capital gains tax? Is it desirable to move them early and pay the tax anyway? These are complex questions, and the answer will depend on individual circumstances, but for many individuals there will be interesting tax planning possibilities.

It is reasonably sure at any rate that the FIF, CGT and FLP rules mean that continued investment into Australian assets by someone planning to move offshore is unlikely to be the most tax-efficient strategy.

Individuals who have significant 'active' non-Australian business income, may be able to make use of offshore corporate tax shelters. They will need to give careful thought to how to structure this income once emigration has taken place, to ensure that it will not remain within the grasp of the tax authorities. Above all the structure selected must remain legal, not only as far as you are concerned, but as far as they are too.

Australian Resident Planning to remain in Australia

The Australian Tax Office (ATO) has done quite a thorough job of catching the income or capital gains from just about every kind of offshore or foreign investment that residents can get involved in. Tax is either applied as gains are made, or they are applied when an investment is realised, with taxes being calculated back over the period of the investment and compounded forward to the time of payment.

Almost all foreign source income held in straightforward individual ownership, is taxed under the FIF, CGT, FLP, CFC or general anti-avoidance rules and it is normal for income to be taxed as it arises and not when distributed. It's evident that any increased returns that may be possible from offshore investments, may be eaten away by greater costs of capital, and possibly by higher tax rates. Resident Australians

The "How To" of Global Investment

have to be very careful before making offshore investments. How you structure your investments is all-important, but as you will see throughout this book, there are things you can do.

Although Australian citizens may still choose to set up offshore trusts, the rationale should be asset protection and investment opportunity rather than tax minimisation. Trusts are caught by the legislation, as much as other types of investment structure, and should be considered as tax-neutral at best.

As far as investment income is concerned, international tax planning for Australian residents is concerned with providing investment structures which are fiscally transparent, so that the gains from higher-yielding international or offshore investments can be taxed in the investor's hands on the same basis as domestic investments. Other than for mutual fund investments, this usually means employing limited partnership or limited liability company structures, which are provided by many offshore jurisdictions, which are usually un-taxed in the offshore jurisdiction, and which are treated as fiscally transparent by the tax authorities.

Individuals who have significant 'active' business income may be able to make use of offshore corporate tax shelters.

Australian Businessperson or Executive Working Offshore

A foreigner becomes resident in Australia for tax purposes if he stays more than 183 days in the jurisdiction within any tax year, or if he has Australian domicile (meaning, behaves generally as if Australia is his permanent base). Australia has double tax treaties with many other countries, which often include "tie-breaker" clauses to deal with double tax-residency situations.

An Australian tax-resident is subject to Australian tax on his or her world-wide income, from the time Australian residence is begun. The taxation year of immigration (ending 30th June) is divided into two parts: the non-resident part in which only Australian-source income is taxed, and the resident part, which is fully taxed. Non-residents are taxed only on Australian-source income.

Non-Australian property acquired after 1985 and owned at the time of immigration is deemed to have a fair market value on the date that Australian residency has begun. After 1985, it is subject to Australian CGT if you dispose of it during residency at the value it was on your

The Offshore Investment Guide

arrival. However, if you cease Australian residency, it will be deemed sold at that time and the CGT will still apply.

This rule can be hurtful, although the "5-in-10" concession exempts assets held by anyone who has resided in Australia for less than 5 out of the previous 10 years on their departure. Most short-term expatriate workers in Australia will benefit from the 5-in-10 rule, but anyone who might stay more than 5 years in Australia must be extremely careful about assets acquired prior to taking up residence, or during residence.

The "5-in-10" rule does not apply to assets acquired during Australian residency, but on departure it may be possible to elect that an asset acquired during residency should be treated as Australian, so that it is taxed only on final disposal and not on departure, but this is a gamble on future Australian tax rates.

Taxable income includes income from personal services (employment or business), bonuses, interest, dividends, rent, royalties, trust distributions and most types of capital gain (on assets acquired after 1985). Foreign-source income which has been taxed usually attracts a tax credit up to the amount of Australian tax that would have been payable. Foreign "passive" income (ie dividends, interest, royalties etc) is treated as a separate class of income, and tax credits are segregated according to class.

Since interests in many types of domestic and offshore trust are subject both to CGT and income tax, it is necessary to take good professional advice on such interests before taking up residence in Australia. It may be possible to bring forward distributions, to postpone them, or to distribute trust assets among family members, all in order to minimise the possibility of incurring Australian taxation during residence.

The same reasoning applies to grants of stock options, which are taxable events in Australia, and should probably be brought forward to occur before immigration takes place.

There is a danger that an offshore entity (trust, company or whatever), if controlled by an individual becoming resident or by his family group, will be considered to be Australian, and subject to tax on its world-wide income. The 5-in-10 rule is not available to companies. The ownership structure of offshore (and all foreign) assets must be carefully checked out in advance.

Regarding shareholdings in foreign and offshore companies, Australia has fairly severe CFC (Controlled Foreign Corporation) rules, which apply to closely-held companies (where 5 or fewer resident

The "How To" of Global Investment

shareholders control 50% or more of the shares) and result in taxation of the company's income whether distributed or not.

Australia also has FIF (Foreign Investment Fund) rules, which apply income taxes to the increase in value of non-controlling holdings in overseas trusts and companies, if their income is mainly passive (i.e. it catches mutual funds and similar types of investment). There is an equivalent rule applying to Foreign Life Assurance Policies (FLP rules).

There are a number of exemptions from FIF and FLP taxation, including one for people holding a residence permit for less than 4 years, which will apply to most short-term expatriates, and one for investments totaling below $50,000. The calculation basis for the FIF tax is quite complex and can be onerous for the funds concerned.

Trusts which are not caught by the "control" or FIF rules, may yet be caught by more general provisions, under which Australian-resident individuals are also taxed on their non-controlling interests in certain types of trust, on an accruals basis – i.e. on the annual increase in fund value, whether distributed or not.

Income "franked" under any of these three sets of rules is, however, exempt from further Australian taxation on the income taxed to the level of the franking.

To those of you who are wondering what "franked" means, it simply means "Tax-Paid". However, it doesn't mean tax fully paid, it could mean partially paid, as it depends on your personal tax rate. Often dividends paid in Australia are franked to 30% (the corporate tax rate) but many people who pay in excess of this level, will then have to top it up to their own tax level after taking into account the 30% already paid. Simple?

Currently, there are no death or gift duties in Australia - one thing the incoming resident doesn't have to worry about. But it's nearly the only thing!

The Situation for Americans

American Resident Planning to go Offshore

Because the US taxes its citizens on the basis of their nationality and not on the basis of their residence, the concept of 'offshore' is not very useful to a US national from a residence point of view. There is an income tax concession available during non-residence, but beyond that the only real option for a US citizen is to change nationality. In all other

The Offshore Investment Guide

respects the international tax situation of an individual citizen is about the same, whether they are in or out of the US.

Individuals who have significant 'active' business income may be able to make use of offshore corporate tax shelters, including the foreign sales corporation (currently under threat from the WTO).

Non-Residence US expatriates who meet the Physical Presence Test (you spend more than 330 days in a foreign country in a given year) or meet the Bona Fide Resident Test (you are a bona fide resident of a foreign country or countries for an uninterrupted period that includes at least a whole tax year), get a deduction of $76,000 of foreign earned income, and possibly some deductions related to housing costs. If you pay foreign taxes, it may be possible to offset these against US taxes, if there is a double tax treaty with the country in which you are resident.

American Resident Planning to stay in the USA

The IRS has done quite a thorough job of catching the income or capital gains from just about every kind of offshore or foreign investment that US residents can get involved in. Taxes are either applied as gains are made, or they are applied when an investment is realised, with taxes being calculated back over the period of the investment and compounded forward to the time of payment.

Some of the key tax collection mechanisms are aimed at Controlled Foreign Corporations, Foreign Personal Holding Companies, Foreign Investment Companies, Passive Foreign Investment Companies, Grantor Trust Provisions and Foreign Trust Reporting Requirements.

Although US citizens may still choose to set up offshore trusts, the rationale should be asset protection rather than tax minimisation. Trusts are caught by the legislation as much as other types of investment structure, and should be considered as tax-neutral.

As far as 'passive' income is concerned, international tax planning for US residents is, therefore, concerned with providing investment structures which are fiscally transparent, so that the gains from higher-yielding international or offshore investments can be taxed in the investor's hands on the same basis as domestic investments. This usually means employing limited partnership or limited liability company structures, which are provided by many offshore jurisdictions, which are usually un-taxed in the offshore jurisdiction, and which are treated as transparent by the IRS.

The "How To" of Global Investment

Straightforward investments into public offshore investment funds, which may offer superior returns to domestic funds, will be caught by the Passive Foreign Investment Company legislation, and it will often be correct to make an election, in order to pay tax, year-by-year, on the fund's increase in asset value (excluding unrealised capital gains).

Individuals who have significant 'active' business income may be able to make use of offshore corporate tax shelters, including the foreign sales corporation.

American Businessperson or Executive Working Offshore

The US taxes foreign nationals based on a residence qualification, using a 3-year formula totaling the number of days in the current year plus one third of the number of days last year, and one sixth of the number of days in the previous year. If the total is more than 183, you are a tax resident, and this applies whatever your visa status (a complex question in itself, not easy to deal with here).

Tax-resident foreign nationals in the US are taxed just about on the same basis as a US national, that is to say, on their world-wide income, comprehensively defined. There are tax credits under double tax treaties for some foreign tax deductions.

Unfortunately, the offshore investment options are not very interesting, indeed your existing offshore investments may fall under US tax laws, so that you are well advised to take professional advice on your situation before becoming tax-resident in the US.

Under US PFIC (Passive Foreign Investment Corporation) legislation, gains on disposal of your holdings, in almost any kind of offshore or mutual fund are likely to be taxed as income, spread over the years in which you held the investment.

Trading activity in shares while you are US-resident may quite possibly bring on capital gains tax or income tax charges, depending on where and how the acquisitions were made. You are not likely to be able to make use of the various pensions-related tax-breaks for share acquisition available to US citizens, unless your residence is for a long period; and at the same time, you will almost certainly not be able to obtain tax deductions for US tax purposes on continuing contributions to pension plans in your home country.

All in all, it will probably be best for you to make sure that existing offshore investments do not mature and are not disposed of during US

The Offshore Investment Guide

residence, and that any new investments will not need to be changed and will not mature until after US residence has ceased.

You also need to be aware that a long period of US residence, particularly if close to retirement, may mean that the IRS will continue to have an ability to tax you after you have ceased to be US-resident.

In the light of all the above, it can be seen that professional advice is even more than usually essential for anyone contemplating US residence, or thinking of carrying on an investment activity while a US resident.

The Situation for the British

British Resident Planning to go Offshore

There is a considerable difference between permanent and temporary non-residence.

Temporary non-residence

An individual spending a limited period overseas (e.g. a diplomat or a business executive) will probably be in a favourable income tax situation during non-residence, but 5 years of non-residence is required before capital gains tax ceases to apply to asset sales, so there is not much point in trying to transfer or cystallise assets offshore unless a very long absence is in view. Offshore assets acquired during non-residence will have the same status as those acquired during residence, so there is no extra advantage to be gained from offshore investment due to non-residence as such.

Permanent non-residence

There are various types of offshore investment available to UK residents, which are not liable to tax until they mature or are cashed in, and it is clear that if this takes place after a move into a low-tax area, then UK tax has successfully been avoided. This may even be true of a move into another high-tax country, because the UK tax regime for offshore investments is worse that that in most other high-tax countries.

Once a firm decision to move offshore has been made, careful thought should also be given to existing UK capital assets, including pension assets. The UK government has recently relaxed its position on pension transfers overseas, meaning that it is now possible to make transfers out of UK company schemes to overseas schemes more easily. The

The "How To" of Global Investment

Inland Revenue has also confirmed, that if you belong to a stakeholder scheme, and subsequently become non-resident, you can continue to contribute for up to 5 years. However, in the event that you choose not to return to the UK, your pension income can end up fragmented. This is a complex area, which needs careful consideration in terms of your personal circumstances.

It is reasonably sure at any rate that continued investment into UK assets by someone planning to move offshore is unlikely to be the most tax-efficient strategy.

British Resident Planning to Stay in Britain

Offshore investment bonds are available to UK residents in various guises, allowing deferral of taxation until maturity, when the penalty will be taxation of the whole gain as income. Even with recent relaxations in the capital gains tax regime, these bonds may still be attractive for some individuals.

Pension investment can also include an offshore element, although in the UK the tax advantages of pensions have been steadily eroded, via other tax-efficient investments, which are more flexible. In particular, for high earners, the pension provision over and above that allowed for tax purposes, can be invested in an offshore Funded Unrecognised Retirement Benefit Scheme (FURBS). However, the Inland Revenue has so far refused to give these investments 'pension' status. The non-UK life assurance sector has been particularly innovative in these types of product.

Inheritance tax can be a major consideration for UK residents, and offshore trust structures remain one of the best ways of mitigating or completely avoiding the tax. There is plentiful information available on this subject from UK financial product providers.

British Businessperson or Executive Working Offshore

The UK is no tax haven, but it does have relatively low tax rates compared with some other European countries, and it offers exemption from tax for income from foreign investments, for people who are resident, but not domiciled in the UK. For expatriate executives with assets to invest, a UK posting or residential base therefore offers very good tax planning opportunities.

Foreign investment income is exempt from tax for such individuals, as long as the income is not remitted to the UK. Therefore they can safely

The Offshore Investment Guide

make offshore investments, knowing that the income will be reinvested without deduction - the ideal way of turning income into capital without taxation.

American citizens, and nationals of the very few other countries that tax world-wide income on the basis of citizenship, won't be able to take advantage of this UK possibility, but for all other nationals, it is available.

The best type of offshore investment may depend on future residential plans. Many countries tax world-wide income based on residence, and if a return to such a home jurisdiction is planned, then investments should probably be made through trusts or other tax-distancing vehicles. If a return is planned to a home tax regime, which fixes only on domestic source income (the case for many or most offshore jurisdictions), then direct investment is safe enough.

Some Offshore Investment Rules

- It is Not Illegal for you to invest offshore
- It is Not Illegal for you to approach offshore funds
- It IS illegal for offshore funds to send a prospectus to Australia, the US or the UK

The "How To" of Global Investment

Investing Offshore

To many investors to invest "offshore", is to take risks, risks that you may think are unnecessary or of no real value, but this is simply not true.... on both counts. The risks are no greater than onshore investing and there is great value in investing offshore. In this chapter I'll show you why.

First let me point out the insignificance of the Australian Market. It represents just 1.2% of the total world market. Do you seriously think this is where the best opportunities are available... or do you think that you may be missing out on something?

> **It's better to earn 25% Offshore and Pay Tax, rather than earn 10% here and still pay tax!**

If you think you are missing out, you are right!

Let me show you something here. If you had invested purely in the Australian share market, your returns would have been around 7% for the last 10 years. If you had invested in:
- The USA it would have been 15%
- Europe it would have been 14%
- The UK it would have been 9%
- The European Union countries it would have been 14%

The Offshore Investment Guide

> The difference between say 7% and a return of say 14% in the bigger scheme of things? Well, it's not only double the return, but with compounding, it will triple your return in the longer term!

So, as you can see, if you had diversified into these markets you would have done better. Now, you may think, what is the difference between say 7% and a return of say 14% in the bigger scheme of things?

Well, it's not only double the return, but with compounding, it will triple your return in the longer term. It could be the difference between retiring extremely well and relying on some sort of government benefit to top you up.

The Insignificance of the Australian Market

As I mentioned earlier, the Australian market is only 1.2% of the total market, but I think it would be interesting to look where all the money is in the world markets.
- The USA represents 46%
- Japan 14%
- The UK 9%
- France 5%
- Germany 5%
- Switzerland 3%
- Canada 2.5%
- Netherlands 2.5%
- Italy 2%
- Spain 1.6%
- Hong Kong 1.5%
- The rest.....6.7%

In that 6.7% we have India, Russia, China, all the rest of Europe, Singapore, Korea the rest of Asia and all of South America.

As you can see, to take advantage of the real growth and dominant areas of world markets you should be looking at North America, western Europe and Japan for starters.

The "How To" of Global Investment

Diversification into global markets offers many advantages

One of the questions, that often enters the minds of investors is, "Why do other markets out perform ours and will that be the case in the future?"

The answer to this question is in two parts. The first dealing with "Why do other markets out perform ours?"
The Australian market is very limited in respect, that there are market sectors we no longer have representation in, which from time to time "boom". For instance:
- Aerospace Technology (Boeing or Airbus Industries))
- Major pharmaceuticals (Pfizer or Bristol Myers)
- Heavy Engineering (General Electric)
- Vehicle Manufacture (GM or Daimler Chrysler)
- Large Scale Food Manufacture and processing (Nestle)
- Electrical and Electronic manufacturing and technology (LG or Sony)
- Software and Computer Development (Microsoft or Intel)
- Mobile Phone Technology (Nokia)
- Military Systems (GE or EADS)
- Chemicals (Monsanto or Dupont)
- Consumer Products (Proctor and Gamble)
- Semiconductors (Intel or Vitesse)
- Restaurant Chains (McDonalds)
- Major Biotechnology (Mylan, Merck or Amgen)
- Major Financial Services (American Express or Citigroup)
- Medical Supplies (Johnson and Johnson)
- Conglomerates (GE or Honeywell)

And there's probably a few that I've missed. It makes you wonder what we do here in Australia? It's a somewhat limited list when you are looking at companies that can compete on the world stage, but here goes:
- Mining (Rio Tinto)
- Oil (BHP Billiton)
- Media (News Corp)
- Building Products (CSR)
- Logistics (Brambles)
- Banking (NAB)
- Airlines (Qantas)
- Telecommunications (Telstra)
- Property Development (Lend Lease)
- Property Management (Westfield)

The Offshore Investment Guide

- Rubber Goods (Ansell)

In the case of the global companies above, there are many alternatives for investment in these sectors. In addition, they are all truly global companies operating in many markets.

This is not the case with the Australian companies. These 11 companies are about it when it comes to "global" companies based in Australia. Of these, only News Corp, Qantas, Lend Lease, Westfield, Rio Tinto, BHP and Brambles could be considered up with the leaders in their sector. That means, if your plan is to diversify into global markets, it comes down to about 7 companies in Australia who do it on a global sense and even then I'm stretching it with Lend Lease and Westfield, seeing they only operate in one or two other markets, albeit successfully. Now, I'm not trying to run down Australian companies, but when we only have 1.2% of the market, what do you expect?

> **The market in Australia is so small that it can only provide growth equivalent to GDP growth or population growth**

When considering "Global Markets" and the companies that operate in them, they do have the advantage of always being in the right place at the right time and can experience growth not possible when a company is confined to one small market. The market in Australia is so small that it can only provide growth equivalent to GDP growth or population growth.

When global companies review their expansion, they have many new markets, including emerging markets, to consider. Look at Microsoft as an example, their products have been used worldwide, in fact you can't think of a country where Microsoft would not be a market leader, but when Eastern European countries begin to integrate more with their Western counterparts, Microsoft will see a steep increase in computer usage. This will occur also in Central and Eastern Asia, South America etc. So, you can see the potential for Microsoft is enormous, whereas, it's hard to see one local company, being in a position to dominate world markets like this. Again, this is a compelling reason to invest into global or offshore markets, and not necessarily Microsoft either, I was just using them as an example.

Now, to the second part of the question, "Will that be the case in the future?" Well, I suppose we have pretty much answered that question already. The answer is obviously "yes". The Australian market is a mature and "well exploited" market with few growth opportunities, serviced by mainly "inward looking" companies that really don't consider

The "How To" of Global Investment

international markets and their growth seriously. The reason for this is, generally lack of expertise and capital shortages, for such a large commitment.

Ways to Invest Offshore

If you are convinced that Offshore or Global Investing is something to consider, there are several ways to invest. They range from "full on" investments to "stick your toe in the water". Let's have a look at ways to get yourself invested in global markets.

- You can invest in the companies I listed earlier, that were Australian Companies operating in international markets.
- You can invest in International companies that are listed on the Australian Stock exchange and this list is rather short with a few notables being Newmont Gold and Phillip Morris.
- You can invest in International or Global Funds run by Australian Fund managers. I am sceptical about this because nearly all of them under perform their respective indices. This shows a serious lack of ability and knowledge by local fund managers............... All except one, and they are outstanding when you consider their returns, Platinum Fund Management in Sydney. All of their funds outstrip all the indices, regardless of how you look at it.... Bloody brilliant! They are listed in the back of this book in the Investment Contacts chapter.
- You can invest directly into International shares via a broker offshore, via the Internet brokers available, or even your local broker. You may need to use a larger, more sophisticated broker for this purpose. I have listed some who can help you in the back of this book in the Investment Contacts chapter.
- Finally, you can take advantage of the management skills of some the best investment gurus in the world by investing in specialist offshore funds, that have achieved amazing results over the years. How about these few as an example of what has been going on "behind your back"?
    -Prosperity CUB FD The yearly return has been averaging 120% for the last 5 years
    -AHL Currency Fund has been returning 53% per annum over the 10 years
    -Cambrian Fund has averaged 110% per annum over the last 10 years

I could list stacks more just like these ones too. Now compare that to what you have been getting from your fund manager or superannuation fund...... Makes you wonder what they are doing with your money doesn't it? Your fund manager is making a fortune out of you and your

The Offshore Investment Guide

money and you are being given lousy returns and because you have no access to anything better, you stay put. They have a jolly old time ripping fees and administration costs out of your fund and they

It makes you wonder what local fund managers are doing with your money when they are able to achieve such pathetic returns

don't even have to make a profit! I should exclaim an expletive at this point on your behalf right now….. &*%$#@!. How's that?

There is no reason to continue with this, now you know what's possible. It's time to make a change on what you do with your money.

My two High Yield Investments books can help you get started. They are updated on a regular basis and the figure quoted on the funds above, were correct as at September 2003.

There is an order form at the back of this book.

And just to get you started……………..

I have compiled 4 offshore funds that have performed well over a long period of time. While they are not the top funds by any stretch of the imagination (the best ones are in the books above), they are certainly not slouches. They conform to the requirements of Quality and Growth.

- **Man-AHL Diversified PLC** – Has returned 21.5% per annum since 1996. Contact: www.maninvestmentproducts.com. No front-end load (Front end load is where a fee is charged upon entry into the fund); declining redemption fees starting at 3% for the first two years following purchase declining to zero after seven years.
- **GAM Diversity** – Has returned 13.2% per annum since 1989. The euro share class (offering currency diversification) is GAM

The "How To" of Global Investment

Diversity Euro Class. Contact: www.gam.com. 5% front-end load, 0% redemption fee.
- **Pioneer-Momentum All-Weather Fund** - Has returned 9.3% per annum since 1995. Contact: www.momentumuk.com. 5% front-end load, 0% redemption fee.
- **SocGen International Sicav** - Has returned 12% per annum since 1997. Contact: www.sgam.fr. Front-end load up to 3%.

Investment Concepts You Should Understand Before You Begin Investing

"What is the best way to create or invest a large lump amount of money?"

So much depends on variables in respect of needs, objectives, individual circumstances and willingness to accept risk, or as it is better defined, "volatility".

The basic problem is the overwhelming choice of options! Government Securities, Equities, Options, Bonds, etc. Most available investments have a worthwhile value under certain circumstances. The trick is to "establish the circumstances".

Then, and only then, can you start the elimination process to come up with decent investments. This process involves attention to three areas:

1. Your willingness to accept risk.

2. Your objectives

3. The time scale

Willingness to Accept Risk
In fact total loss of capital is not a realistic possibility for most of the investments, that a private investor would be looking at yet, to most people, risk means the possibility of total loss. "Volatility", much better describes the risk associated with investment. For example, a particular investment might double in value over three years but, after the first six months, it might have halved. So, the end result is extremely satisfactory, but this is no good to you, if you have panicked at the six month point and sold the investment at a 50% loss.

> **Can you live with volatility in the interest of longer term potential?**

Can you live with volatility in the interest of longer term potential (which

131

The Offshore Investment Guide

might not materialise)? If so, how much volatility can you accept? If not, then you must sacrifice "potential" extra returns in the interest of peace of mind.

Your objectives

Of course, we all have the same objective, 25% pa returns with little or no volatility!

However, in the real world, objectives boil down, quite simply, to income, growth or a combination of the two.

If you have maximum income and no potential for growth, then you are locking into a gradual decline in your standards. This is simply because, inflation will erode the value of both your income and your capital. I will show you an example of this a little later.

The Time Scale

The longer one leaves an investment, the greater the potential for growth. Many people recall the stock market crash of 1987, but very few remember what happened for the whole of the year. In fact if you were invested in the US or most European Markets at the beginning of the year and still in by the end, you would still have shown a profit.

Those who invested at the top of the market in 1987 and are still holding today would have seen some tremendous returns.

Volatilty within equities will always remain. The usual warning we hear- that share prices can fall as well as rise, is not just a possibility. It's a certainty!

The next thing to consider is "broad sectors" of investment.

Broad Sectors

Basically, there are 3 broad investment sectors. These are:-

Cash

Generally speaking, Cash is, or should be, all about liquidity, i.e. to cover short to medium term capital expenditure, so that longer-term investments can be kept in place.

The "How To" of Global Investment

When Cash is treated as "invested capital" rather than liquidity, there is a very serious downside and this is where there is no potential for growth of the invested capital.

Long term Cash holdings will be constantly devalued by the effect of inflation. For instance, at a modest annual inflation rate of 5% the buying power of $1000 is reduced to $377 over a 20-year period and, at the end of the day the only relevance to money is, what it will buy.

Thus the "cautious investor" who uses this sector exclusively is not "risking" the decline of his capital. He is guaranteeing it.

Cash as an investment, and this includes cash management accounts or funds, is useless and shows a lack of imagination and a lack of investment understanding.

Middle Ground Investments

These are holdings which aim to produce better medium to long-term results than Cash, but at lower levels of volatility than Equities, therefore, they are not no risk but they are low risk and medium/long term returns can be expected to be somewhere between those of Cash and Equities. This is the realm of the "safe" or "cautious" investor.

Equities and Managed Funds

This is the sector, which has always produced the best results in the medium to long term, thus offering potential capital protection. A study by BZW shows, that the average yearly return on shares since 1918, has been 7.8% after allowing for inflation. This compares with 1.4% from Cash, i.e. shares have produced an average return of 5 times more than Cash for over 75 years!

However, nothing is perfect and equities are no exception. The downside, is short to medium term volatility. Values can change quite alarmingly in the short term. This causes inexperienced investors to "cut and run" thus turning a "paper loss", which may have recovered, into a "real loss". Big mistake .... Huge!

Equities should be treated as medium to long-term investments and only medium to longer term money should be committed to them.

> Cash is what I would call a "parking space". Don't leave your money there because when you get back, it will be "vandalised and the wheels will be missing" - Inflation being the culprit!

The Offshore Investment Guide

In summary, Cash offers liquidity and security in the short term and is what I would call a "parking space". You don't leave your money there too long because when you get back to it, it will be "vandalised and the wheels will be missing" - Inflation being the culprit.

Equities can be volatile in the short term, but the level of volatility in relation to the original investment, may reduce in time.

A Middle Ground approach gives you a mixture of the two. Reduced volatility and reduced returns.

However, everyone has different needs, objectives and attitudes and the eventual portfolio must match the particular individual. Also much depends on the amount under consideration.

Most private investors will use "collective investments" such as Offshore and Mutual Funds, Unit & Investment Trusts and Insurance Bonds. When you choose these correctly, you have the benefit of the manager's expertise.......... there is just two things to remember and they are:

- Quality
- Growth

Quality and Growth

Consider that $1000 invested for 10 years, achieving an annual compound growth rate of 8%, will grow to $2159. If the growth rate is 10%, it will grow to $2594. So, a seemingly insignificant difference of 2% pa generates an end result 44% better, in terms of the original investment.

The way to achieve that difference, is to ensure that you only buy "quality and growth". Unfortunately, finding "quality and growth" isn't as simple as it seems. In this process, there are a few aspects to consider before investing to ensure you are getting Quality and Growth, or at least the potential for growth.

They are:
- Does the fund have a 3, 5 or 10 year history of good returns? – this demonstrates the potential growth factor
- Does the fund manager have most of their funds performing well? – this demonstrates the quality of the manager

The "How To" of Global Investment

- Are the underlying investments good ones, that make sense to you? Are they investing in good quality equities with good growth potential?
- Is the Fund Manager aggressive? What I mean here is, is the manager active in the markets trading and taking profits? short selling when opportunities arise? do they hedge their currency positions? do they cover risky positions with call and put options? The other type of manager, is a "buy and forget" investor that may not achieve the sort of returns that might interest someone wanting extraordinary returns.

Lots to consider? Well, there is, but if you do your due diligence you will be well rewarded financially. I'm not saying you'll get it right all the time, I don't, but you'll end up doing better than most investors.

Best Time to Invest?

When the Australian dollar is high. This will mean your money will buy more investments offshore when they are converted to foreign currencies

---

A Word of Warning!

I have just told you when to invest.... When the A$ is high. However, there is a downside.

- If you invest when the Australian dollar is high and then after you invest the dollar drops..... you'll make money even if the investment doesn't go up..... great!
- If, however, the Australian dollar rises after you have invested.... You'll lose money..... ouch! But hopefully if this arises and you have invested in the right place, any currency exchange loss will be offset by a capital appreciation rise in the value of your investment.
- Beware of Emerging Markets.... They can turn into submerging markets and cause chaos to your portfolio. Always allocate only small amounts to the risky area, until you really understand the market you are investing in.

The Offshore Investment Guide

Another Word of Warning!

When investigating Offshore Investment opportunities make sure you do your due diligence thoroughly...... please. But to give you a helping hand in this area, I'll tell you what NOT to invest in.

- Invest in nothing that proclaims to be a Rollover, Bank Debenture or Trading program. The warning signs are:
    1. If you are asked to sign a confidentiality agreement or
    2. They offer monthly returns that sound like good yearly returns.

    These are all scams.... 100% of them, no exceptions, regardless of who is telling you, or how glossy the brochure is. The people promoting them are liars and cheats and I would have them all shot at dawn if I had my way. Anybody promoting these schemes should be reported to the authorities immediately! In Australia, the ASIC, and in the US, ring the SEC.
- Never invest with anybody who rings you up out of the blue and claims to be with a broker offshore... or an investment manager. These are "boiler room" scams and they too are liars, cheats and thieves. Again, I would have them shot at dawn!
- Do the fund or investment managers operate from a normal and regulated country and this includes the better Offshore Financial Centres?... If not "run away"
- Anything offered from Thailand.... Keep running!
- Anything offered from Africa (Nigeria, Gambia, Kenya etc)..... Keep going!
- You can read more about these scams and plenty others in my book, Scams and Frauds – Financial Crime Exposed!

The Biggest Mistake People Make

Without a doubt, one of the biggest mistakes people make when it comes to investing, be it offshore or otherwise, is not to understand that just a few percentage points can make the difference between a mediocre retirement or living and a fantastic one.

The Rich have known for years that to squeeze an extra few percent out of their investments makes all the difference. It really does.

I'm going to show you three examples of what you could do with a lump sum of $500,000 in retirement.

The "How To" of Global Investment

The first is what so many conservative investors do.... They put it into Cash, like a Cash Management Fund. It's hard to believe, but they still do it. I'll show you why this is the biggest mistake investors make.

The second is a more broad-minded investor with an medium to longer term investment outlook. He's decided to invest in Australian Shares through one of the better fund managers.

The last investor, understands the value of offshore investing and has invested in 3 offshore funds. We use actual examples that are in my High Yield books, so we're not being too hypothetical here.

Each investor has a requirement of $1,000 per week to live on, which is a pretty comfortable living, but not too comfortable. So, we need $52,000 per year. We assume no tax is payable in any of the scenarios because everybody's tax situation is different, so we'll work in pre-tax figures only.

Let's see how they go!

Investor 1 – Cash Management Fund

Year 1

Starting Balance $500,000
Add: Interest Earned $500,000 @ 4% $20,000
Less: Living Expenses   -$52,000
End of Year Balance $468,000

Year 2

Starting Balance $468,000
Add: Interest Earned $500,000 @ 4% $18,720
Less: Living Expenses   -$52,000
End of Year Balance $434,720

Year 3

Starting Balance $434,720
Add: Interest Earned $500,000 @ 4% $17,389
Less: Living Expenses   -$52,000
End of Year Balance $400,109

This isn't looking good is it? Do you know what? As long as this investor doesn't mind dying in year 14 everything will be fine.... Because all the money is gone after 14 years.

The Offshore Investment Guide

What's worse is we haven't even taken in to account inflation, of say 4-5% which means he actually would have been broke after about 10 years and then in the real world there would have been tax, and this would have brought it back to around 7 years.

So you can see what I was saying earlier about Cash investments is correct. Not a good idea!

Investor 2 – Australian Shares through a Managed Fund

We'll assume a higher than average return that can be expected from Australian shares, but let's say you have a very good fund manager. Their returns have averaged 10%pa.

Year 1

Starting Balance	$500,000
Add: Gross Return $500,000 @ 10%	$50,000
Less: Living Expenses	-$52,000
End of Year Balance	$498,000

Year 2

Starting Balance	$498,000
Add: Gross Return $500,000 @ 10%	$49,800
Less: Living Expenses	-$52,000
End of Year Balance	$495,800

Year 3

Starting Balance	$495,800
Add: Gross Return $500,000 @ 10%	$49,580
Less: Living Expenses	-$52,000
End of Year Balance	$493,380

As you can see this is a much better way to invest, but you are still going backwards and you will run out of money eventually. While it doesn't seem too bad, it will accelerate as the years go by and inflation and tax will just kill you and you'll be in a pretty bad way in around 20 years.

The "How To" of Global Investment

Investor 3 – Offshore Investment through Managed Funds

This investor has decided to invest in the following funds:

- Platinum International Fund @ 20%pa (long term average) $200,000
- Schroder Ventures International Fund @ 29%pa (since inception) $200,000
- Finsbury Worldwide Pharmaceuticals Trust @ 40% (since inception) $100,000

Now, based on our $500,000, this gives us an average return of 27%pa. I could have picked funds with returns over 100%pa, but I thought let's be conservative here, & came up with something really achievable.

Year 1

Starting Balance	$500,000
Add: Gross Return $500,000 @ 27%	$135,000
Less: Living Expenses	-$52,000
End of Year Balance	$583,000

Year 2

Starting Balance	$583,000
Add: Gross Return $500,000 @ 10%	$157,000
Less: Living Expenses	-$52,000
End of Year Balance	$688,000

Year 3

Starting Balance	$688,000
Add: Gross Return $500,000 @ 10%	$186,000
Less: Living Expenses	-$52,000
End of Year Balance	$822,000

The balances for each year will be as follows:

Year 4	$992,000
Year 5	$1,208,000

You're a millionaire now!

Year 6	$1,481,000
Year 7	$1,830,000

The Offshore Investment Guide

Year 8	$2,272,000
Year 9	$2,833,000
Year 10	$3,546,000
Year 11	$4,452,000
Year 12	$5,602,000
Year 13	$7,063,000
Year 14	$8,918,000
Year 15	$11,274,000 Yippee!

So, you have gone from broke in 7 to 20 years to being a multi-millionaire! Just because you chose, a more risky, but incredibly more lucrative investment choice.

> **Do you think Offshore Investing is something you should consider in your portfolio?
> Can you afford not to?**

The Offshore Investing Process

This is where many people stall in the whole "Offshore Investing thing". They are convinced they should invest....... But how.... Where.... When....With who?

"Ah! ..... All too hard!" It's easy to give up, but would you want to?.... now you have seen what is possible?

Well, to help you and make sure you don't give up, we'll go through the setup process step by step.

The "How To" of Global Investment

What you will need

Your are going to require:

- An Offshore Bank Account
- A Maildrop Address
- A Broker
- And, possibly a Company and/or a Trust..... but we'll get to this one last.

An Offshore Bank Account

This is the first step in the offshore investment process. In our chapter, Banking Issues, we discussed several options you have. We talked about a Swiss banking option as well as the procedure to open an account.

In my book Invisible Banking and Invisible World you'll find many banking options in almost all Offshore Financial Centres (OFC). Each OFC has its own advantages and disadvantages depending on your circumstances and requirements. To try and fit all that into this book would be well beyond the scope of this book. I suggest you refer to either of these two books or even my Offshore Banking Directory CD which lists hundreds of offshore banks and gives you their contact details.

A Maildrop Address

The reason you need one of these is because Offshore Funds will not send you information in Australia, USA or the UK. Simply because it is illegal for them to do so. It's not illegal for you to receive and act on it, only for them to send it.

A maildrop is simply a place offshore where you have an address for mail to be sent. The companies that operate these simply redirect all mail to you in Australia by placing all the mail received in your "box", putting it all in a large plain envelope and airmailing it to you when ever you want it. Very simple process.

The idea is to have a maildrop in a county that has no restrictions as far as what is sent to it.

One that has been recommended to me is in Vanuatu.

The Offshore Investment Guide

The company is South Pacific Express and their website is www.southpacificexpress.com

Mailing address is:
Accounts at South Pacific Express
PO Box 1692
Port Vila
Vanuatu
South Pacific

Phone: +678 41409

Physical Address:
Deouma Rd
Port Vila
Efate
Vanuatu
South Pacific

Email: info@southpacificexpress.com

Stephen Mundi - Manager
Email: steve@southpacificexpress.com

Below, I have reproduced their Frequently Asked Questions so you can find out a little more about what they do:

How often is Mail Forwarded?
For Regular accounts mail is forwarded on the Friday of each week. For Premium accounts this can be done daily if required.

What is the difference between Regular and Premium membership?
Premium account entitles the forwarding of mail on a daily basis if required and also includes the option for courier deliveries to be arranged when time is of the essence

Regular account entitles the forwarding of mail on a weekly basis either bundled or separately but does not allow for same day forwarding or the use of a courier.

Do you open my mail?
No SPE never opens any mail. When we receive it we place it into another envelope and either on forward it on the day or bundle it with others depending on prior arrangements and account type.

The "How To" of Global Investment

Why would you bundle the mail?
The reason for this is to save you money. As in many cases 4 or 5 letters bundled could be sent for the price of one.

Can you accept delivery of couriered packages and parcels?
Yes, we accept delivery of parcels from couriers, as many investment opportunities will send their prospectus via a courier.

Can you arrange a courier to deliver my documents or package if required?
Courier delivery service is only available for Premium account members.

What articles of mail will you not accept?
There are laws and regulations surrounding the sending of mail that must be obeyed.
Postal services in general prohibit the sending of the following items:
Illegal Explosives
Destructive Items
Live Materials
Guns
Drugs

Please Note: Anything that is even remotely associated to the manufacture of drugs and amphetamines will be detected and seized by customs. In the event of such an incident occurring the offending account will be cancelled immediately and full cooperation with the authorities will be rendered.

Can you sign for documents if required?
SPE can sign for documents only when it is addressed to you care of South Pacific Express.

What names can I have the account in?
You can have your account in whatever name you choose whether it be an individual or company name or even the name of a trust or self managed superannuation fund.

What will my mailing address be?
The PO box number below is an example only and not the actual number.

John Citizen
PO Box 350
Port Vila
Vanuatu
South Pacific

143

The Offshore Investment Guide

Couriers won't deliver to PO boxes so how can you accept couriered deliveries?
For couriered deliveries a physical address is given.
In this way couriered packages may be accepted

Who uses a Mail Drop or Mail Redirection Service as you call it?
Traditionally people wanting privacy or anonymity used mail drops. Whether seeking to keep their affairs secret from governments, or colleagues of spouses.

At South Pacific Express we believe that our clients use our services for very different reasons than those stated above and that is to have an international mailing address so as to access investment opportunities in a cost effective manner.

Do you guarantee that the mail will get to me?
Unfortunately we cannot guarantee that you will receive your mail, as international postal services are not within our control. We will however guarantee that all mail received by SPE belonging to valid account holders will be sent.

How much does your service cost?
Regular Accounts cost $400. This is broken down into $300 for account set-up administration and PO box and a further $100 mail bond, which covers the postage.

Premium Accounts cost $560. This is broken up into $400 for account set-up administration and PO box and an account with the courier company. The remaining $160 is for the mail bond as the couriering of documents is considerably more expensive.

Can I change from an existing regular account to a premium one?
Yes simply arrange to pay the difference and it's done

Are these prices charged annually?
No the prices quoted above are one off joining fees

What are your annual charges?
Standard accounts renewal fees are $122

Premium Accounts renewal fees are $174

How long is my account valid for?
All accounts are valid for a period of 12 months from the time you join.

What happens when my mail bond money runs out?
You will be notified when your mail bond is at $50 and again when it

The "How To" of Global Investment

reaches $20.
In the event that your mail bond reaches zero any mail received will be held until the bond is toped-up.

What happens if I still have money left in my mail bond at the end of 12 months?
Any money held in the form of a mail bond will simply be rolled over into the following 12 month period providing you renew your membership.

How much do you charge for forwarding my mail?
All mail is charged at twice the postage. This covers stamps envelopes and labor. However this is nowhere near as expensive as you may think.

For example:
Imagine that 10 letters are bundled and posted to Australia for a cost of $3.00
when our agent receives the mail they place a 45cent stamp on each envelope and post them.

You would pay 10% of the $3.00 being 30 cents and double the 45 cents being 90 cents.
So in reality you would pay $1.20. In other words $1.20 would be deducted from your mail bond.

This is only an example and may vary.

What is your charge for couriered documents?
With couriered documents this is a free service to our premium account holders and you are only charged what the courier company charges.

What currency do you charge in?
All prices quoted are in Australian Dollars

Why do you use Australian Dollars if you are in Vanuatu?
As Australia is the largest westernized country closest to Vanuatu we chose to use their currency.

The two other reasons are:
1) Not many people know that the Vatu is the currency of Vanuatu.
2) Having prices quoted in Vatu makes them look prohibitively expensive for example $400 Australian dollars equals 30,000 Vatu.

What types of payment do you accept?
At present we accept payment via:
American Express
Master Card

The Offshore Investment Guide

Visa
or if you prefer personal, bank cheque or money order.
This company will work in well with the broker I'm going to tell you about.

The Broker

One of the things I am often asked is, "Do you know a good broker that can help me with some of the funds you mention in your books?"

Landau Securities in Vanuatu can assist you with the purchase of around 95% of available offshore funds.

The man to speak to is Endre Dobozy, he is an expat Australian and is an authorised agent and is permitted to deal in the securities offered.

Contact them via their website at www.landausecurities.com

Phone Number: + 678 238 39
Mobile Number: + 678 438 39
Fax: + 678 27 847
Email: info@landausecurities.com

Postal Address
Landau Securities
PO Box 316
Port Vila
Vanuatu
South Pacific

Physical Address
Landau Securities
Teouma Road
Port Vila
Vanuatu
South Pacific

Do you need a Company or Trust?

There has been a lot written about this. Some people say you need to have a company or trust and they are …. Right! Others have said that you don't need to have a company or trust and they are right too!

The "How To" of Global Investment

The truth is, whether you need a company or trust depends on what you are trying to achieve.

Let's look at the two types of offshore investors:

Type 1 – No Company or Trust Needed

These investors simply want to invest offshore and diversify their portfolios. They are not interested in tax benefits, asset protection or privacy so much, just the investment returns.

Their requirements are:
- Investment returns available only by investing offshore
- Currency diversification
- Offshore banking

To achieve this, they need to have the following:

- An Offshore bank account
- A Maildrop address
- A broker

Type 2 – Company and/or Trust Needed

These investors are looking at the bigger picture. Not only do they want good returns, but they want to protect their money by employing asset protection strategies, as well as maximizing any tax benefits that may be available to them legally.

Their requirements are:
- Investment returns available only by investing offshore
- Currency diversification
- Offshore banking
- Asset Protection with the use of a Company/trust structure as explain in the chapter, **Asset Protection and The Nasty World of Litigation**
- Financial Privacy and Confidentiality
- Possible Tax Benefits

To achieve this, they will need to have the following:

- An Offshore bank account
- A Maildrop address – Not really needed as your incorporation agent will normally include this as part of the wider services they provide
- A broker

The Offshore Investment Guide

- A Company formed
- A Trust Formed

If this is you, and you are looking at going "whole hog", then I recommend you speak to the people listed below and read my book, The Invisible World.

Incorporation Agent

ILS (Isle of Man) Limited
2nd Floor
Atlantic House
Circular Road
Douglas
Isle of Man
IM1 1SQ

Telephone: +44 1624 682500
Fax: +44 1624 628488
E-Mail: iom@ils-world.com

Sample of Services:
For detailed information on our services please select from the following:
- Incorporation
- Client Administration
- Corporate Validation Services for Banks
- Corporate Products
- Trusts
- Banking
- VAT Services
- Guide to Billing & Charging

The ILS Group, established in 1973, is a world leader in the provision of tax-efficient international corporate services. We establish and administer corporations and trusts almost anywhere in the world.

The "How To" of Global Investment

Offshore for Different Reasons

Whilst this book mainly focuses on the typical investor seeking opportunities offshore, and while I realise that will constitute 90% of the readers, I thought I would also cover the realities of doing other types of "investing" offshore. It may be real estate or business for instance.

The Real Estate Investor

Domestic Real Estate

Real estate investors could benefit by holding his or her properties in an offshore company. This is permitted in all tax havens except Luxembourg. Benefits, for example, are: not only do you achieve ownership anonymity, but you gain savings when it comes to transfer and stamp duty costs (and in some circumstances possibly reducing capital gains tax) by the owner of the company selling the shares in the company which is a foreign asset, instead of the property itself.

This means if you want to sell a property, you simply sell the company to the buyer. As far as anybody is concerned, the property is still owned by exactly the same offshore company. It's only the ownership of the company that has changed. Keep in mind this company does not have to be registered in Australia, because it is exempt from registration, if all the company does is hold property.

Just ensure, if you wish to do this, keep just one property per company otherwise, it makes it difficult to sell the company, if you only want to sell one property. The buyer would also be able to achieve the same beneficial situation in the future and would benefit by not having to pay stamp duty in the first instance as in reality, the property has not changed hands. It could be argued that, if you owned or controlled the offshore company, any capital gains made on the sale of the offshore company's shares could be assessable for tax purposes in your home country.

The Offshore Investment Guide

International Real Estate

If you are in the right place at the right time, investing in real estate can be one of the most profitable and enjoyable forms of medium to long term investment there is.

> **Diversifying your investment portfolio by buying property in several different countries, for example, can help to cushion you against downturns in any one particular market**

Depending on your circumstances, international real estate investment may prove preferable, for a number of reasons, despite the additional challenges it can sometimes pose. Diversifying your investment portfolio by buying property in several different countries, for example, can help to cushion you against downturns in any one particular market. Even if you think you cannot afford to do this, you may find that you will be able to snap up an incomparable bargain in an up-and-coming country, which would never have been available in your country of residence.

Now, if you decide that international property investment is for you, there are several different ways of going about it. Those with neither the time nor the inclination to become landlords, or who simply want to diversify a top-heavy portfolio, might choose to invest indirectly, using one of the many real estate related funds available. (A top-heavy portfolio is one where you have a high percentage of your money in a small number of investments.)

Ground rent funds, for example, are proving increasingly popular with investors, and offer a relatively low risk and secure investment with the possibility of high returns. As with all mutual fund investments, there are specific advantages and disadvantages, but if you are interested in the growth possibilities in this market and would prefer a less 'hands on' approach, then this may be for you.

On the other hand, you may not even have an investment portfolio - you may just be looking for somewhere nice and sunny to retire to. Or you may be an expat looking to supplement your income. Or you might have been relocated by your employer, and need somewhere to live. Or... well, the list goes on. There could be any number of circumstances, both personal and financial, driving you to consider investing in property overseas. In this article we will deal with the issues raised by international property investment, and the possible taxation implications raised by such purchases.

The "How To" of Global Investment

International mortgages - Do I need one?

One of the primary considerations, when purchasing property either domestically, or on an international level, is raising the necessary amount of money. Unless you happen to have enough ready cash just lying around, chances are you will need to take out a mortgage. There are several options:

1) Taking out a mortgage with a local bank. You may, however, find yourself constrained by exchange control rules (where they still exist). Even in jurisdictions where exchange controls have been lifted, such as Spain, you may find that domestic banks and building societies will charge non-resident foreign nationals higher rates of interest.

2) Taking out a mortgage or loan from a bank or building society in your country of origin. This is difficult, as most lenders will only lend on properties in their jurisdiction.

3) Taking out the mortgage offered by the developer. Sometimes, with new complexes, developers will offer their own mortgages in order to increase sales

4) Taking out a mortgage with an international institution. Even if you are confident in your understanding of the processes involved in purchasing property in your country of choice, this is probably the most sensible option, for the simple reason there are likely to be issues involved in dealing with an expatriate client, which a local provider may not have the expertise to cope with.

There are a growing number of international mortgage brokers and relocation specialists offering international products, tailored to meet the needs of expatriate property investors. Although it is possible to go it alone, you may find that enlisting the services of a professional company experienced in dealing with international markets, eases a purchase considerably. They are likely to be well versed in the processes and legislation applicable to non-resident purchasers, and can often mediate between yourself and the local entities involved. Ideally, having a relationship with a bank in the same country as you are purchasing the property is advantageous.

Borrowing Money for Offshore Property?

You must borrow the money from a lender in the same country as the property – The reason? They won't lend you the money unless they have control of the property and that means within their reach.

The Offshore Investment Guide

What sort of mortgage?

There are several different sorts of mortgages available, so you should really shop around to make sure that the international mortgage broker or bank you choose to handle your affairs offers a wide range of products, from a varied group of international providers. Below is a basic rundown of the different types of mortgage available, although not necessarily all for your country of choice, so you need to check:

1) Repayment mortgages. With this type of mortgage, you pay a little of the interest and a little of the capital off each month, so that at the end of the term, the debt has been repaid completely, and the property is yours. Although in the early years, very little of the capital is repaid, as the amount of capital owed decreases, so does the amount of interest which accrues, so towards the end of the term there is a kind of 'snowballing effect' in terms of the amount of capital which can be paid off at a time. This is generally considered the safest bet in terms of mortgage loans, although it is usually more expensive than an interest only mortgage.

2) Interest only mortgages. With one of these, your payments to the lender simply pay off the interest on the loan, and the capital is paid off at the end of the term. Monthly payments are (obviously) lower than they would be for a repayment mortgage, and the idea is that you put the money you save on repayments each month into an investment fund, so that by the time the term ends, you will have accumulated enough to pay off the mortgage. Or that's the theory. If your investments do well, you could be in a position to repay the mortgage early, or have some money left over at the end of the term. However, in order for that to happen, your investment fund needs to bring you returns, which are higher than the interest you are paying on your mortgage, otherwise there will be a shortfall at the end of the term. This is something for sophisticated investors only, unless you are very disciplined.

3) Endowment mortgages. These used to be used quite a lot in conjunction with interest only mortgages. They are designed to guarantee that if you die before the end of the term, the mortgage will be repaid, and to provide a means of paying off the capital owed at the end of the term. However, there is no guarantee that an endowment will repay the loan in full at the end of the term, and as with many pensions and life assurance products, there are high 'front-end' costs. Where there is preferential tax treatment for life assurance premiums they may still be of some use, but as the majority of expatriates are excluded from the benefits of domestic superannuation investment, they are rarely suitable.

The "How To" of Global Investment

Usually, international mortgage providers will offer both repayment and interest only mortgages at fixed, variable, capped and sometimes discounted interest rates, all of which are fairly self explanatory, and have specific benefits and disadvantages.

International home-owning - The logistics.....

Several of the problems you may encounter, if you decide to purchase property in a country, other than that in which you are resident, are likely to be logistical. Okay, so you can afford to take time off to find a property in your country of choice, and maybe even visit a few times a year, but that is likely to be all. This is where designated international organisations come into their own.

For example, in Spain, the completion of a mortgage must take place in front of an appointed notary, and all parties to the purchase including the vendor, lawyers, the buyer, and a representative of the lender. However, if you are unable to be there due to previous commitments (or simply geography!) an international broker should be able to help you obtain a power of attorney, allowing someone else to sign on your behalf.

Renting your property out when you are constantly on the move can be a bit of a headache, but hiring a letting agent, qualified in dealing with international clients could take the pressure off. They can help you find suitable tenants, prepare a letting agreement, take the security deposit, deal with utilities bills, collect the rent (the important bit!), visit the property on a regular basis, check empty properties, and undertake property maintenance during a tenancy.

Costs

Ignoring taxation (which we will deal with in more detail later), and quite apart from the cost of the mortgage itself, there are other expenses to bear in mind, when arranging a mortgage for your investment property, and these vary considerably from country to country. For example, in France, the fee level can be affected by the age of the property (as newer properties attract lower charges), the number of people involved, and how many outside agencies (e.g. estate agents, lawyers, brokers, letting agencies) are involved.

If buying a property in France, (over and above the broker's fee) you should be prepared to pay:
- A land registry fee of 0.6% for property under 5 years old, or a 1% fee for anything older

The Offshore Investment Guide

- The notaire's sales commission of up to 5% (where an estate agent is not used. If an estate agent is used, their fees are usually paid by the seller of the property).
- Stamp duty of 0.6% for property under 5 years old, or a 6% (yes that figure is right!) charge for anything older.
- The notaire's conveyancing fees, which vary according to the value of the property, but can be anything from 1-1.5%.

As previously stated, costs will vary depending on the location of your property. As you can see the issue of additional expenses needs to be taken into account when deciding whether international property investment is for you - although the returns can sometimes be spectacular - it's not cheap!

The tax implications of international property investment
Although the majority of countries impose some kind of taxation on international property investment by foreign nationals, it would be a rare (and unpopular) country, which levied all of the above. The tax implications of your foreign real estate investment will vary in complexity and impact, according to where it is located, and to a certain extent, what you intend to do with the property when you have purchased it. As a general rule, in the majority of countries, if the tax authorities believe that the purchase was made as a 'commercial' investment (i.e. if you habitually buy, renovate, and sell on, or if you have bought undeveloped land with a view to building a housing complex or leisure facility), they will view you as a property dealer, and tax your investment accordingly at a higher rate.

Where taxes are levied on international property investment, they will usually fall into the following categories:
1) Taxes on the purchase, acquisition or transfer of the property or land, such as capital acquisitions tax, stamp duty and property transfer tax.
2) Taxes on the ownership of and/or residence in the property, such as local and national property taxes, and land tax.
3) Taxes on rental income. (If you choose not to live in the property, be aware that there may be additional taxes imposed on non-resident or foreign landlords. Not necessarily devastating, but still a factor to be considered, if buying to let overseas.)
4) Taxes on disposal of the property, such as capital gains tax, gift taxes, and death duties.

As previously stated, property taxation regimes vary widely from country to country, and you may feel that low, or no-tax jurisdictions are the ideal choice for you. However, in some cases (although not all), property investment opportunities are limited only to the very wealthy, who must be willing to contribute substantially to the local economy, and

The "How To" of Global Investment

purchase luxury real estate. Other jurisdictions limit the number of foreign nationals permitted residence or work permits, in order to maintain the standards of living, and protect the employment chances of existing residents.

Governments in non-tax haven countries, tend to impose fewer restrictions on property purchase for investment or residential purposes by foreign nationals. However, in such countries, the likelihood is that you will face more taxes on your investment. Some property investors choose to purchase international property via an offshore company or trust in order to bypass some of the taxes levied in high tax countries, and although this can be a valid option, it is not suitable in all circumstances. We will discuss this in more detail later.

Where you decide to purchase property is, in the final analysis, a personal choice, and will need to be based on your circumstances, resources, and eventual goals. If you have your heart set on retiring to a beachfront house in the Bahamas, you are unlikely to be satisfied with a one-bedroom apartment in Cyprus. If, however, you are looking to subsidise your income by providing affordable housing to expatriates and other professionals, the latter would be ideal. It all depends...

I hope I haven't frightened you off with all of this talk of fees and taxes because you will often find that international property can be purchased very cheaply compared to expensive cities like Sydney and Melbourne.

Also, when the Australian dollar is high is an ideal time to invest offshore.

What do you use, an offshore Company or a Trust?

I'll keep this bit very simple........It is probably best to use the "asset protection" model in the Asset Protection chapter. With a property you need to protect it, as it is such a substantial asset. I would, however, recommend that you use one trustee company but use a new trust for each new property under the company. This, as I mentioned earlier makes selling the trust, rather than direct selling the property, an easier option, one that has its advantages.

So, Is it worth it?

The answer to this question, will depend on your personal circumstances, what you hope to achieve by investing, and how much you can afford to spend. There is a vast spectrum of opportunities available within the property investment field, ranging from the ridiculously expensive to the nicely affordable, and with the help of an

The Offshore Investment Guide

international broker or lender, you should be able to find something suited to your tastes and pocket.

Investing in a 'real' asset, as opposed to an intangible one can sometimes provide more stability, and property tends to hold its value better than other commodities. However, capital growth could be questionable. Also, a property is an investment that you can't easily get rid of if you need to, so keep this in mind. Equities etc are far easier to offload in a hurry.

You also need to be aware of the "health" of the property market you are in, and possible fluctuations in interest rates and inflation that can affect the value of your investment.

The Business Person

> **What is the number one fear of the small businessman? ....Being sued and losing everything**

There are many reasons why someone either in business, or contemplating being in business should consider the available offshore option. Now, it may not suit all businesses, but there certainly are some businesses that are superbly suited to using offshore options. However, tough new regulations can curtail much of what you thought you could do and you should be aware of what you are faced with, and know that it's not that simple. This section of the book hasn't been put together to convince you to go offshore, but to inform you of what is possible (legal) and what is not (illegal). I wish I could tell you that you could do more, but times are changing.

Now, you may be thinking that the only reason to setup offshore, is to reduce tax but in reality, tax is not the major benefit in many cases. Asset protection certainly is, these days anyway.

What is the number one fear of the small businessman? Being sued and losing everything. Think this is a bit far fetched? I read recently about a group of gypsies that make a living out of suing supermarkets in the US. You think I am kidding, right? They have false social security cards, sometimes three or four of them. They "fall down" in supermarkets, and then they sue. They are so sophisticated, they even know which supermarket chains have better liability insurance, and what insurance companies they use. This is important, because they try not to file too many claims with one insurance carrier, to reduce suspicion.

The "How To" of Global Investment

It's very unfortunate that there are people out there that do this sort of thing. It's even more unfortunate that they are successful with the legal system. Even worse, they get away with their scam. While they are doing this in the US, how long before some "sleazes" do it here? Also, what if your insurance company doesn't pay, or you're underinsured etc. You could be ruined. They sue your business, then come after you for the rest.

The point really being, if a supermarket chain, that can afford both "top of the line" insurance and barristers to defend them in court...... can be sued and lose.........what chance do you think you have? The answer lies in being broke. No one ever attempts to sue a homeless person. Even if they sue, and the court awards them $100,000, how and what are they going to collect?

I am not suggesting you become homeless, just make sure your business never has any assets and that you have nothing to take personally either. How? Get it someplace safe, legally - preferably out of the country where it cannot be "attacked". Also make sure your business leases everything from another "company".

There are people in this world that use loop-holes or just take advantage of the stupidity found within the legal system, in order to take your money away from you. Why not use that same legal system to protect yourself?

Looking at an offshore presence is not such a silly thing, particularly if you are in a high-risk category. Let's look at some of the areas of business that could utilise an offshore presence:

- **International Trading**

Export and import transactions can be facilitated by the use of offshore companies. The use of an offshore company between a seller and a buyer of products or services in different countries can allow profits on the transaction to be accumulated offshore. An offshore company can be designated as a marketing or an export consultancy.

Invoicing is via the offshore company, but goods can normally travel direct from source to destination. Keep in mind though, that transfer pricing is frowned upon, by many tax authorities around the world, so manipulation of prices on a non-commercial is best avoided.

The Offshore Investment Guide

- **Manufacturing and Distribution**

Some countries, like Ireland, have a preferential tax rate for manufacturers and this can be exploited by establishing a manufacturing company in Ireland, or separating off the manufacturing part of a company's operations.

Many countries, including the Dominican Republic, Labuan and Dubai, have special "free-zones" in place to encourage foreign business to "set up shop". Some of the benefits to a company operating out of such a "free-zone" are: Zero corporate income tax for 15 or 20 years, reduced costs for services (such as trash collection & electricity), greatly reduced labor costs (minimum wage of 80 cents per hour), duty free import of raw materials & equipment needed for the business, and duty-free export of finished products.

In addition, many countries have very favorable trade agreements with many countries with respect to reduced or even zero import tariffs on goods entering those markets. In fact, based on this alone, if you are currently exporting a product to Europe from Australia, US or Canada, you could possibly reduce or eliminate the duties you pay to the countries you are exporting to, just because your product is now coming out of the Dominican Republic, for example. In effect, by simply changing your address, you could possibly save money, and be able to reduce the retail sales price of your product, making it more competitive.

- **Consultancy and Services**

Consultants and those providing services such as musicians and entertainers often receive much of their income from overseas. And as you well know, most entertainers these days have an offshore base.

This income can be remitted to an offshore company, which in turn employs the consultant and pays over a modest amount for expenses, whilst retaining the bulk of the moneys offshore.

Employment overseas is often facilitated by the use of an offshore employment company. This can either employ an individual or a group of individuals working overseas. The employee keeps the bulk of his income outside the country of employment and the structure can also reduce currency exchange problems.

Be aware of your tax obligations here, as far as earnings from employment offshore, as has been talked about earlier in the book.

The "How To" of Global Investment

Intellectual Property

Patents, copyrights, trade marks, franchises and other rights such as those in music, computer software and technical know-how can all be transferred into the ownership of a licensing company, which may be offshore or onshore. Licence or franchise agreements are made by the offshore company and royalty payments and licence fees are received by the company.

Withholding tax will normally be payable on distributions from the licensing company, but the effects can be minimised by the use of double tax treaties.

Internet Trading and E-Commerce

One of the fastest growing areas of international trade is the Internet. The international nature of the trade and the potential tax complications of dealing internationally, can be solved by the creation of a specialist Internet trading company offshore, however it may not be quite this simple.

To obtain favourable tax treatment, it is necessary to locate the server physically offshore and to have a separate domain name. However, as I mention a little later, depending on the residency/citizenship of the owners of the business, there may be a tax liability anyway.

It is often expressed that such operations are "all in cyberspace" and therefore location is not important. In fact, regulation is increasing and planning should anticipate likely future controls.

Let's look at a couple of examples of what might typically happen in a "cyberspace" situation.

A German company sells porcelain dolls via mail order. The company factory is in Germany. They have a printed catalog, and a web site, which is domiciled on a server in Gibraltar. People from all over the world make purchases via the Internet. It stands to reason that being based in Germany, the company would in fact have a German corporate income tax liability, but what about elsewhere? If citizens of Australia make purchases of this company's product, does that mean that the company must file a tax return with (and pay taxes to) the Australian Government?

Taking this a step further, A Bahamas company markets magazine subscriptions over the Internet. Since the Bahamas company, is, in fact, an "IBC" and as such does not market to or do business with Bahamian

The Offshore Investment Guide

citizens, the company has no tax liability in the Bahamas. If the company web site is domiciled in the Cayman Islands, and customers make purchases, which are in effect done directly in the Bahamas, to whom does the company have a tax liability? If the Cayman government said, that no tax liability was due to the Cayman Islands because no Cayman citizens were customers and also there was no company business (receipt of payment, shipment of product, etc.) being done in the Cayman Islands, to whom does the company have a tax liability? On what basis does the company have a tax liability if commerce is done in "cyberspace"?

The reality of these examples is quite clear, as far as tax authorities worldwide are concerned. The tax liability lies with the owner of the company domiciled in the tax haven. For example if that is you, or a trust or company you control/own/direct, then you are liable under the FIF (or similar) legislation in place.

So, if you are planning something offshore in this vein, you must do some careful planning, with your tax adviser and your incorporation agent, before embarking on anything. It's just not as simple as it used to be............. mmmmm?

If you are interested in exploring the options of e-Commerce, the incorporation agent who seems to be up with it and can obviously help you is International Law Systems. Here are their details and a little bit of information they have provided on their service.

ILS (Isle of Man) Limited
2nd Floor, Atlantic House, Circular Road
Douglas, Isle of Man, IM1 1SQ
Telephone: +44 1624 682500   Fax: +44 1624 628488
E-Mail: iom@ils-world.com

Information from ILS:
Through ILS's association with Micronet, a leading offshore Internet Service Provider based in Jersey, we are able to offer clients tax-efficient e-commerce solutions.

The ability to structure and operate an e-business offshore is no different in practical terms, than setting up an offshore trading company and certainly the tax considerations are very similar. One of the requirements of operating an e-business in Jersey, is that the website itself is owned by a Jersey company and the authorities have agreed that the Jersey International Business Company (IBC) is the appropriate vehicle. Thus, once we have created the IBC we host the website on one of our servers, (which are physically located in Micronet's Jersey premises) and we provide the directors of the IBC and actually

The "How To" of Global Investment

administer the day to day running of the company. We maintain the website and ensure that it is stable, we clear payments as they arrive in Jersey and provide accounting services to the company, in the same way we do for our traditional clients. In addition, we are in the process of developing a cost effective multi-currency payment solution and are also able to assist with the design and implementation of the website.

Because we are involved with the development of the business and the actual management of the Jersey IBC, we can ensure that the company is resident in Jersey. The hype that e-commerce is tax-free because Governments around the world do not have appropriate legislation is a myth, but with careful structuring we can provide a legal, tax efficient solution.

> The information in The Business Investor section should not be considered tax advice, as the information given is not country specific. You should consult your legal or tax advisor, as well as ILS before doing anything.

The Asset Protector

For the investor interested in Asset Protection as their prime concern, please read the chapter Asset Protection and The Nasty World of Litigation.

The Equity & Fund Investor

For the investor interested in Asset Protection as their prime concern, please read the chapter Offshore Investing

The Offshore Investment Guide

International Investment Contacts

This is the chapter where I give a way some of my "secret" (and not so secret) sites that I get some valuable information from. I'm sure some of them will help you too.

ASIC

http://www.asic.gov.au

The website of the ASIC is very handy when doing your due diligence. Their 'Fido" site is where you'll find lots of juicy information on scams.

Atlas Offshore

http://www.atlasofoffshore.com/

An extensive but easy to use site, with numerous sections covering all aspects of living and investing offshore. There is a vast section dedicated to links to offshore banks, whilst the offshore investing area of the site covers a wide range of topics including mutual fund providers, offshore trusts and global investment news. If time is no object, there is plenty of additional information to be had here.

Bahamas B2B

http://www.bahamasb2b.com

Bahamas B2B provides a range of useful B2B business and e-commerce resources for the Bahamas. There are tools and solutions for small businesses, an employment centre with a handy 'Find a Job' search function, a Bahamas business directory, and e-commerce tips. A free newsletter is also available.

The "How To" of Global Investment

Escape Artist

http://www.escapeartist.com/

Go to the Offshore Investing section and select Tax Havens to find a website about offshore investments and lifestyles. The two main features of this site, are a drop down list of the individual offshore jurisdictions and a General Resources section. This consists of an alphabetical list of company websites where information from offshore banks, financial planners, consultants and other services can be found. There is also a clearing house providing contact details and a secure contact form for a number of offshore service providers including banks, brokerage companies and tax consultants

Directmoving.com

http://www.directmoving.com

Directmoving.com is the first worldwide relocation portal for both HR managers and expatriates. It offers a wealth of information and resources on many aspects of international mobility, and provides a series of practical tools to be used before, during and after relocation. Directmoving allows expats to buy a variety of services online, including international health insurance, hotel reservations, plane tickets, car rental, etc. It is a site that looks good.

Expatexpert.com

http://www.expatexpert.com

Expatexpert.com offers a range of information and advice, for international expatriates, covering areas of expat life such as careers, repatriation and family life. The site also has links to other expatriate resources and goods and service providers.

Expat Financial

http://www.expatfinancial.com

Expat Financial provides a user-friendly service for expatriates, brokering insurance and financial plans, and providing a range of other services. These include tips for expatriates living abroad, articles on expatriate financial products, and a links section which is a useful resource for expatriates of all nationalities with an interest in related sites.

The Offshore Investment Guide

Expat Network

http://www.expatnetwork.com

Expat Network provides a kind of home base for the UK expatriate community. Although the site was initially designed to provide primarily employment resources, it has now expanded, and in addition to this, provides a whole host of resources on other topics of interest to expats, including lifestyle, travel, and shopping. There is also an extensive categorised links section.

Financial Times

http://www.ft.com

This is the UK's Financial Times website that will provide you with information not only on UK equities and managed funds and investment issues, but also the rest of Europe. A really good site.

Fortrend Securities - Broker

http://www.fortrend.com.au

Fortrend offers a wealth of information on worldwide equities and can assist you to buy them. You can trade over the net or by phone.

Global Investor on the Net

http://www.globalinvestor.com

This daunting-looking site claiming to be the 'complete tool for investing world-wide through the Internet' is surprisingly user-friendly and carries a wealth of information. The site is divided into eight main sections: stock markets, offshore mutual funds, bonds, money market, currencies, commodities, strategies and links to major news sites. The section on offshore funds includes risk/return charts, the 10 largest funds and their performance, selected funds, fund trackers and fund managers with a Web presence, many of which are large European institutions but all offering offshore funds. Money Market deals with the best offshore deposit rates and includes a guide by jurisdiction to offshore banks on the Internet, with a useful summary on what to look for when choosing an offshore bank.

Global Travel Insurance.com

http://www.globaltravelinsurance.com

The "How To" of Global Investment

Global Travel Insurance.com is a sister site to Expat Financial, and focuses more specifically on travel insurance for expatriates and travellers world wide. As well as providing travel and medical insurance, the site also offers web-links of interest to short- and long-term travellers, and a world news section.

Independent Financial Advisers

www.independent-financial-advisors.org.uk

Independent Financial Advisors and Financial Advice Links

Interactive Offshore

http://www.offshore.net/
Interactive Investor International's offshore site promises much but in fact, is not the most inspirational guide to investing offshore, with a singularly unappealing appearance. It features product guides, essentially a one-page summary of offshore banking, deposit takers, offshore trusts and other domains; direct links to the sites of about 10 offshore product providers; a one-page description of each jurisdiction and it touches briefly on expatriate mortgages and health insurance.

International Living

http://www.internationalliving.com

For 20 years, International Living magazine has been one of the leading sources of information and advice about living, retiring, and buying real estate overseas. Their website provides lots of useful resources for expatriates, including relocation and travel articles and support, and links to other expat related resources. Subscribers to IL can also pick the brains of 'Mr Savvy Traveller' their resident expert.

Kiplingers

http://www.kiplingers.com

My favourite US investing magazine. Lots of good info on US stocks and funds.

Motley Fool

http://www.fool.com

The Offshore Investment Guide

The Motley Fool website gives you an alternative look at investing in the US market with tips and general investment information.... A pretty good site.

Offshore Rebates.com

http://www.offshore-rebates.com

Offshore-Rebates.com is an online discount brokerage, offering full advice and substantial discounts on a range of major offshore funds and hedge funds. The website provides quick links to mainstream fund providers and also weekly updated reports and commentary from major asset managers. There is also a useful resources page for expatriates. All responses are personal and ongoing service is primary. E-mail invest@offshore-rebates.com for details.

Offshore Today

http://www.offshoretoday.com/

A very new resource, launched by Shorex in March 2000 and updated daily but as yet incomplete. An impressive and easily navigated, offshore finance and online information center, which includes a quarterly magazine with news, analysis, country profiles and offshore careers. The database of offshore investment services and business opportunities are not yet available, but are promising sources of investment providers.

OECD

http:// www.oecd.org

The website of the OECD is full of helpful information on individual countries as well as changes effecting the offshore world.

OFS (Asia)

http://www.ofsasia.com
OFS (Asia) offer a range of services and facilities for international investors and expatriates. These include advice on financial planning, links to financial and investment services, and advice on subjects such as offshore banking and investment techniques.

Smart Money Magazine

http://www.smartmoney.com

The "How To" of Global Investment

Another favourite US money magazine of mine. Lots of US equities information.

TD Waterhouse - Broker

http://www.tdwaterhouse.com.au

This broker can assist with the purchase of US and European market shares, as well as give you access to their research information.

Morgan Stanley

http://www.msci.com

All around the world, funds compare themselves to a variety of MSCI indices. This where you'll find all the information about them.

Morningstar

http://www.morningstar.com

Morningstar provide detailed information of US mutual funds.

Turtle Trader

http://www.turtletrader.com

The turtle trading course takes a trend-following approach to investment, providing long-term investment strategies. They have been online since 1996, and their site, as well as providing information about the course, has extensive free resources for the beginner or expert trader.

Wall Street Offshore
http://www.wallstreetoffshore.com
Wall Street Offshore provides access to over 1000 mutual funds from big name firms such as Janus, Fidelity, and Morgan Stanley Dean Witter. In addition to the offshore mutual fund supermarket section, their website offers a whole host of resources useful to investors. These include up-to-date business headlines, general information about offshore mutual funds, an offshore glossary, and several useful and relevant investing links.

The Offshore Investment Guide

Due Diligence for Offshore Investors

Over the years, I can't tell you the number of people who have told me their woes of investing offshore, the money they have been conned out of, the money they have lost on hot tips.... The mistakes they have made. I understand we all make mistakes, and sometimes we haven't really made mistakes, it just that our timing was a little out. You know, when you invest in something and it immediately goes through the floor, even though all the fundamentals pointed to it going the other direction. In this case if you were told to hold, be patient everything would have been alright, but it's always the case, you panic, become disillusioned and sell.......... Then the price goes back up and you curse and promise never to buy high and sell low again! .... The trick is to do it the other way round ☺

Also, I've noticed that a great many investors have a pre-occupation with wanting "hot tips" from newsletter writers, seminar speakers and book writers. We of course, by the most part, don't have any, and if we did, it would be illegal for us to tell you and pretty stupid, because you'll hate us for the rest of our lives if we were wrong...... and we do get it wrong from time to time and this where we should talk about Due Diligence.

Doing your due diligence is where you take the attitude to "Trust Nobody" and find out for yourself if everything you are being told or reading, is correct. This is where you take responsibility for your investment decisions. This is what every astute investor should do. Do your homework! It is ultimately your investment.

However, doing your due diligence is not always easy, particularly for Offshore Investors, where often you are unfamiliar with companies and funds. So, what I'll attempt to do here is to give you some advice and plug you into some very useful Due Diligence Resources.

The "How To" of Global Investment

Due diligence is simply the process of investigating a potential investment. The term is also used in connection with the purchase of a business or real estate and in mergers or acquisitions. All of the investigative procedures, that are used by a potential buyer to evaluate and investigate the information provided by a potential seller, are called due diligence.

When you are contemplating the purchase of shares in a company, you have the freedom to decide how much time and money to spend to investigate and evaluate the company behind the potential investment. This would be dependent on the amount you are investing. Your level of exposure should indicate how much time you allocate to this task. If it is a large investment, take the time to do it properly. It is your money, your future and your security, that you could possibly be throwing away, if you do not do your research.

You should obtain data summaries of financial information on companies from your adviser, broker or even someone like Standard & Poor's or similar services. These services get the information from the quarterly and annual financial statements that are filed with the government agencies (like the ASIC or SEC) and stock exchanges and are certified by independent audit firms, as to the validity of the accounting procedures utilised.

The problem for the offshore investor is that similar information isn't always as readily available, about companies outside your home country who are not subject to local securities laws, simply because they aren't registered there.

Failing to undertake basic "due diligence" can be financial suicide for your money in the offshore investment game, where financial information about companies (or the people behind them) is much harder to find.

Con artists are rarely able to cheat someone who is free of greed or fear. Greed is the emotion that leads us to want something for nothing or to seek high returns on investments with claims of little risk. Greed gives us the motive to be willing to take advantage of another person. Someone once said that "You can't con an honest man". The word "honest" could be substituted for "someone who isn't greedy".

Your single best defense against any potential scam or scheme is to be willing to walk away from the perceived "opportunity" when you smell a rat, never let your greed takeover and consume you. We all want to believe that 20% per month returns exist with capital guarantees, but it's the greed swaying us. When you know that professional investment

The Offshore Investment Guide

managers rarely make more than the returns achieved by the various market averages, you should be instantly suspicious of any offer that alleges to give you the opportunity to get results far greater than those obtained by professional investors.

The second emotion that causes many people to lose money is fear. Nearly every con game or scam tries to encourage a sense of urgency or you lose the opportunity. "You have to move fast, be decisive", say the hustlers and promoters. The fear of losing an opportunity to get something for nothing, causes people to invest without investigating first.

Greed causes otherwise sane people to give their life savings to a total stranger, who is offering the allure of a "special opportunity" to get high returns without risk or effort. Fear often prevents them from even seeking help to recover their money.

> **Greed causes investors to buy at the top of a rising market and fear causes them to sell at the bottom.**

People who are inherently honest don't expect something for nothing. They are immediately suspicious of anyone who offers them an "opportunity" that seeks to take advantage of others. Such people are very hard to trick into some kind of scam or con game.

The greater the potential opportunity in relation to the amount at risk, the greater the potential for a scam and the more time should be taken to check it out. Furthermore, the more urgent the opportunity is, the greater the potential for it being a scam of some kind.

There are real opportunities available in this world, but they usually require a lot of investigation and patience. The promise of easy money is like the odds of winning the lottery. Nothing comes easy, but if you do your homework, others will think it does, for you anyway.

Due Diligence Resources

David Marchant
http://www.offshorebusiness.com
David Marchant is the author and publisher of *Offshore Alert*, an investigative research service that is delivered as a monthly newsletter, combined with a large computer database for subscribers. He is an investigative journalist with a focus on Bermuda and the Caribbean countries.

The "How To" of Global Investment

He has generated a lot of publicity by accusing the Marc Harris organization in Panama of mismanagement of client funds. Then he won a libel lawsuit filed against him by Harris.

He also took issue with the First International Bank of Grenada and has been at the forefront of many exposes of fraudulent investment schemes offshore. In addition to his writing and maintaining his extensive online database, he also provides some investigative services for individual clients.

Offshore Finance Canada
http://www.offshorefinancecanada.com
This bi-monthly offshore magazine publishes the names of various companies or financial institutions that have "... been the subject of warning notices issued by various regulatory authorities for reasons ranging from suspicious transactions to carrying on business without the proper license." They list the name of the company, the jurisdiction where they are located (if known), the source of the regulatory warning, the date of the warning and some brief clarifying comments. They also maintain a web site for the public with the accumulated names from current and past issues of their publication.

Matt Blackman
http://www.goldhaven.com
Matt Blackman is a free lance writer/journalist who writes extensively for a number of offshore publications and he also publishes an email newsletter for subscribers. He maintains a web site for subscribers that is not available to the public but which does include an extensive database of articles about various companies or individuals in the offshore community. His public web site also provides information about various investment scams and schemes on or through the Internet. He is available for private investigative due diligence for investors interested in various offshore investments.

Information on Scam Investments
http://www.quatloos.com
Jay Adkisson is an attorney who has written extensively about various offshore investment scams and schemes being promoted on the Internet. His web site is a compilation of the many articles he has written on the subject and is an excellent place to begin with respect to investigating any potential offshore investment. If an investment looks like a Ponzi scheme or a multi-level marketing scheme or like one of the many illegal tax avoidance schemes, the potential investor should be prepared to extend much greater time and funds to investigate and evaluate the sponsor, promoter or vendor of the investment.
See also my book Scams & Frauds

Conclusion & Putting the Pieces Together

So, by now you may have decided that diversifying some or all of your investment portfolio offshore may in fact be a good idea, or possibly an option worth exploring. We know it's legal, we know it can be profitable, we know it's not all that hard, so the next step is doing something about it.

However, I have just said, the next step is doing something about it.....

"But what?", you may ask. The step by step procedure would be:

- Identify and write down what you want to achieve – Investing, Asset Protection, Business opportunities or whatever
- Next, contact all the relevant people mentioned in the relevant sections of the book and get them to send you as much information as they can.
- Sit down in peace and quiet and read the information and ensure that you understand it, taking into account time delays, costs etc
- Open a bank account
- Contact either the maildrop people or incorporation agent depending on your needs
- If investing, contact our broker
- At this point it's pretty complete

However, all through this process I encourage you to seek competent legal advice, if there is anything that concerns you or you don't understand.

Also, and I'm really not trying to sell books here, however, read my books:
- The Invisible World
- High Yield Investments 1 & 2

The "How To" of Global Investment

They are the best sources of the most accurate information, that is readily available on the Australian market. Make sure that you have the latest editions available by checking with the Trident Press office, or on line at wwww.tridentpress.com.au, as the information has been updated recently and changed drastically over the last few years.

You will find the depth of information, on each of these subjects, in these books invaluable and they go into much greater detail than this book has been able to accommodate.

Do not forget that a couple of hundred dollars investment on books and educating yourself is a small investment, compared to the possibly costly exercise of having consultants do it all for you, or worse losing your investment. It is imperative that you get your personal goals sorted out first before engaging consultants, as this will save you a lot of time and money.

Now, at this point you may think there is only one "blank" that comes to mind readily, and that's "Where?"….. Where do I do all this?

That really is the subject of The Invisible World, a massive 280 pages on it's own, which is why it can't really be covered here. However, I will give a quick rundown of the top 3….. now this is dangerous because everybody's situation is different and what is number 1 for one person may be number 6 for another. It depends on citizenship, residency, tax laws, your time frame, your needs, time zones, banking requirements etc. So please, remember, this is just a rough guide. See The Invisible World for the full run down. Here we go:

The best places for:

Asset Protection.
- Turks and Caicos
- British Virgin Isles
- Panama

Investments
- Turks and Caicos
- Lichtenstein
- British Virgin Isles

Real Estate
- British Virgin Isles
- Gibraltar
- Isle of Man

The Offshore Investment Guide

Business
- Dubai
- Netherlands Antilles
- Madeira

Banking
- Switzerland
- Jersey
- Cayman Islands (equal third)
- Guernsey (equal third)

Also, I should add, for Australians, Vanuatu has been popular. While it has some good aspects it is still a little unsophisticated in the banking area and there really is only one choice, The Bank of Vanuatu. However, things are improving.

Another bunch of "gems" are being developed by the Americans, as far as good all round structures are concerned, namely, Nevada, Delaware and Wyoming……. Are you really surprised the US is cultivating its own "offshore" industry? By all accounts it's pretty good too. The states have quite a deal of power and can tell the feds to "get nicked" in certain areas.

A final word of Taxation……..

Governments around the world are concerned with:

- **Tax Evasion**
- Money Laundering
- Terrorism

In that order!

Don't believe for a minute what you read or hear to the contrary….. it is tax evasion that concerns them most and that is where they are placing most of their efforts. Governments, by their very nature crave ever increasing amounts of money to support their existence and government grows ever larger to make sure they get all the money they can……. So, they can grow ever larger….. to get all the money they can ………and so it goes on….round and round like a merry-go-round!

Anyway, the bottom line is report all that you owe, and pay tax on any interest, dividends, or capital gains you realise overseas. Ensure however, you also get every single deduction you can and

The "How To" of Global Investment

that you structure your affairs, in such a way that your tax liability is legally minimised….. It is your right, regardless of what "they" would have you believe.

Remember what Australian Media Magnate, Kerry Packer once said to the Senate Select Committee on cross media ownership…….

*"If you pay more tax than you have to…….
You're a Bloody Idiot!"*

The "How to" of Alcohol Intervention

that your associates, your friends, or anyone who was mean to you in the "sobering up again" mind needed it. This is your right, regardless of what those associates might have done.

Remember, after a bender or a drug binge, several agents such as those in the book, Sober Conmen—Robbers, Rats, Cheats...

**"If you see more rats than you have toes,
you've bloody lost."**

Investors Guide to Trident Press Publications

Wealth Creation & Offshore Investment Strategy Books

Many people become a little confused as to what books they should purchase and read to find the information they're after seeing we now have almost 30 different publications.

So, to make it easier we thought we would categorise the books so to enable you to pinpoint the information you need. We've also placed them in order of what we think you should purchase and read first, second, third etc.

The Offshore Investor
We recommend:
1. The Offshore Investment Guide
2. The Invisible World*
3. Invisible Banking*
4. The Offshore Banking CD Rom*
5. High Yield Investments 1*
6. High Yield Investments 2*
7. Future Wealth
8. Offshore Companies and Trusts*
9. Underground Knowledge
10. Underground Knowledge 3
11. Things you didn't Know – Underground Knowledge 2
12. Invisible Cash
13. Scams and Frauds – Financial Crime Exposed
14. Tax Haven Report series

Items marked * are all included in our Complete Offshore Wealth Special which also includes the exclusive Trident Offshore Incorporation and Strategy Manual. We recommend you purchase this Special as it provides you with substantial savings.

The Stock Market Investor
We recommend:
1. The Australian Share Market Guide
2. Investing To Win
3. Build Your Wealth Today
4. Future Wealth

The Privacy Seeker
We recommend:
1. The Privacy Report
2. Underground Knowledge
3. Things You Didn't Know – Underground Knowledge 2
4. Underground Knowledge 3
5. For We are Young and Free.... Or are we?
6. Invisible Cash

Money Management and General Investment
We Recommend:
1. Financial Crisis! – How to Avoid Financial Disaster
2. Investing to Win
3. Build Your Wealth Today

The Business Owner
We Recommend:
1. Going Out on Your Own?

The Wealth Builder
We Recommend:
1. Investing to Win
2. The Offshore Investment Guide
3. High Yield Investments 1
4. High Yield Investments 2
5. Future Wealth
6. The Australian Share Market Guide
7. Financial Crisis!
8. Build Your Wealth Today

The Conservative Investor
We Recommend:
1. Investing to Win
2. Scams and Frauds – Financial Crime Exposed
3. The Australian Share Market Guide
4. Financial Crisis!

Trident Press Pty Limited
Po Box 3068, Bangor NSW 2234 Australia
Phone: 02 9543 0406 Fax: 02 9543 0406
www.tridentpress.com.au

NEW RELEASES FROM TRIDENT PRESS

Trident Press — Wealth Creation & Offshore Investment Strategy Books

Underground Knowledge 3
Secrets of Wealth, Privacy & Offshore Investing

Underground Knowledge 3 Features:

- The Ultimate Strategy for Banking In Silence
- How to Disappear.... And Never Be Found! I expose how the "experts" find you and how you can foil them.
- How to fly just about anywhere in the world for around 15% of the regular fare with top class airlines to...I reveal how to do it, and where top get the tickets from.
- A full report of the best second citizenship programs available and how you can get a second passport, legally and at the right price!
- The ultimate real estate source. Where you can buy great properties around the world for under $50,000...... I even show you where you can buy a castle in Europe for this price.... Yes, a 13th century castle, ready to live in! In fact several castles, this country has plenty of them at bargain prices.
- The best Offshore Investment Broker! This broker can assist you to invest in over 1,000 offshore funds easily.
- A Comprehensive Australian Mail Drop Guide, after many readers' requests.
- Carnivore, Echelon and other snoop programs...How to ensure you don't fall victim.
- Asset Protection - The Perfect Strategy!
- The 8 Golden Rules of Anonymous Banking
- Investing in Portfolio Bonds – A Great Idea and not commonly known
- The Best European Banking Options and Secrets
- The Dangers of Caribbean Credit Cards – How to Reduce your Risk
- Hide Your Assets, so nobody will find them.
- The Hidden Desire of All Investors.... And it's not what you think

- Tax Secrets that are totally legal …. these will amaze you, and your accountant!
- The Superannuation Lie Exposed
- Get Returns on Your Investments just like the banks do
- Is someone spying on you? How to find out and how to foil them
- The Absolute 8 Secrets of Great Wealth….. every millionaire has used these strategies
- The Latest Scams and How to avoid them and they are really convincing…. You may have already been taken and not know it.
- Corporate Pirates…. How to Spot them and How to Avoid them….. Any AMP, HIH or Onetel shareholders out there?
- New Anti-Terrorist Laws will give you some grief …. What you can do about them
- Warren Buffett, Super Genius?…. No, just "super logical". We examine the logic and common sense that made this man the richest investor in history and how his simple rules can be followed so easily
- Plus Lots of other "Secret" Information on Privacy, Investing and Asset Protection

Only $49.50 plus P&H
www.tridentpress.com.au

The Trident Offshore Banking Directory

The Trident Offshore Banking Directory gives you access to hundreds of Offshore banks. The banks are arranged in country order and provide the reader with Internet addresses with direct hyperlink access, addresses, phone numbers and brief highlights and features of many of the banks. A must for all those interested Offshore Banking and having a convenient and easy to use Banking Directory. The Trident Offshore Banking Directory comes on a CD-ROM, in PDF file format, ready to use.

On CD-ROM….ONLY $35 plus P&H

www.tridentpress.com.au

To order these New Releases or any of our other books, either go to our website at www.tridentpress.com.au and order securely online
Or, Fax or phone us on Australia (02) 95430 0406
Or, Write to us at:
Trident Press
PO Box 3068, Bangor NSW 2234 Australia

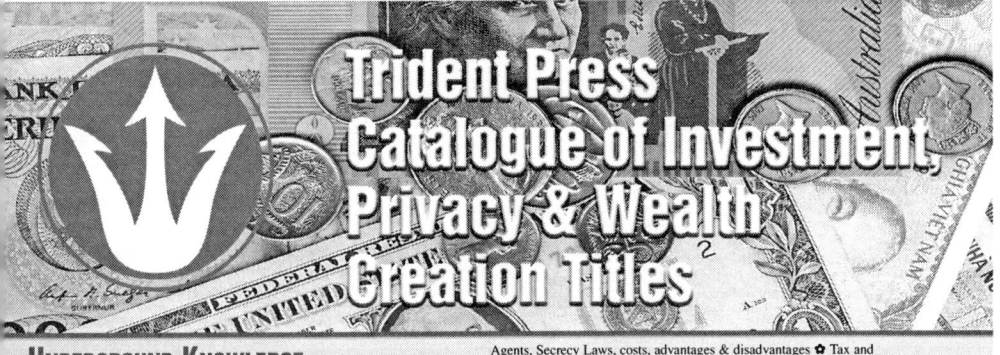

Trident Press Catalogue of Investment, Privacy & Wealth Creation Titles

UNDERGROUND KNOWLEDGE

This is a book that provides valuable and hard to find information - **information your government would prefer you didn't know.** Forbidden information on privacy, money, freedom, technology, special places where freedom is assured, private banking and investing, "big brother" tactics and how to beat them, offshore companies and most importantly, liberty and wealth. Underground Knowledge provides you with information normally reserved for the rich and powerful. Those people in our society that can afford inordinate amounts of money to make more, and secure their privacy. The book provides the reader with practical ways to improve their lives financially and assists the reader to regain their sovereign individual rights. A very unusual and enlightening book!

Features: Privacy, Security, Special Destinations, Technology, Privacy Strategies and Tricks of the Trade, Money Making Ideas, Government Surveillance and how to beat it, plus many more great ideas, concepts and methods to improve your privacy and increase your wealth. **Price AUD$49.50**

I enjoy reading all your books but my favourite was Underground Knowledge - MR, Queensland

I finished your book (Underground Knowledge) last night and it taught me so much. I can't thank you enough for putting this together - it is going to change my life.
- JP, Brisbane

FUTURE WEALTH

Have you ever thought to yourself, "Why can't I have had shares in THAT company?" This is a book that helps that happen. A massive amount of research has gone into producing the book you always wanted, one that more or less predicts the future and informs you which industries are set to boom, which companies you should consider for the future. The book takes the consensus of opinions of economists, analysts, investors, industry experts and gives you definitive answers and solutions.

Features: Future Economics, Globalisation, how to buy high-tech stocks, where the smart and rich have their money, the Internet, the winners and losers of the next decade, and most importantly, *the 53 companies that will be the new industrial powerhouses, their real intrinsic value and how to invest in them.* "If you want to make money, this is the book you need!" **Price AUD$49.50 Latest Edition**

Thank you for your effort in writing very "in-time" publications - AC, Sydney

I wish to thank Lance Spicer for the tremendous books that he has written
- BA, Queensland

THE INVISIBLE WORLD

Financial Freedom & Privacy
Offshore Investment Strategies can be employed to Minimise or Defer Taxation as well as increase your Privacy & Confidentiality
The Invisible World will show you how you can establish offshore companies and trusts to minimise tax and increase privacy as well as take advantage of amazing investment opportunities.

Features: Over 40 Tax Havens are analysed and the book gives you full details of Banks and Incorporation Agents, Secrecy Laws, costs, advantages & disadvantages ✪ Tax and Investment Strategies fully explained in an interesting and easy to read way ✪ Australian Tax Laws explained with loopholes exposed ✪ How to establish your own offshore company or trust privately and inexpensively ✪ How to set up secret bank accounts ✪ Privacy & Secrecy ✪ Second Passports ✪ How Skase beat the system ✪ Investing Offshore - the advantages ✪ Maildrops ✪ Includes new havens and contacts. **Price AUD$59.50 International Best Seller**

Books such as The Invisible World by Australian, Lance Spicer are by far and away the best in the world on this subject (offshore investment) - Amazon.com

I have to congratulate (Lance Spicer) on your writing abilities and educational approach to your financial freedom and privacy series books. You have forwarded everything that I was looking for. It's great stuff and exhilarating to see such a wealth of knowledge and experience delivered in an easy to understand format. Once again, thank you, the information in the Invisible World is priceless!
- Executive, Nortel Networks

GOING OUT ON YOUR OWN?

The Secrets to Small Business Success
This book covers all aspects of small business and shows you practical ways to achieve the results that you desire. In a logical sequence of events, *Going Out on Your Own?* explains getting started, making sure your business will work, right through to proven ways to improve sales by writing ads that work, time management, merchandising, selling, administration and many other important aspects to business success. *Going Out on Your Own?* is the only book that puts together all the information you will need in one inspirational and practical book. Author and accountant Lance Spicer has taken a serious subject and made it entertaining and easy to understand. If you want to be successful in business, you need the secrets and the methods of true business success. *Going Out on Your Own?* contains these secrets and methods. **If you only buy one business book, this is the book. Price AUD$19.95**

I have read through your book and must say I really like the practical advice that you offer in such an easy to read format (Going Out on Your Own?) - Simon & Schuster, Australia

HIGH YIELD INVESTMENTS

The first book published in Australia that details over 60 of the highest yielding investments in the world and how you can invest
This best selling book by Lance Spicer will change the way you invest forever. The book details over 60 of the worlds best and highest yielding investments that YOU can invest in. They are all reliable and most have exceptional track records and international reputations. The investment opportunities exist offshore as well as some right here in Australia. All investments have passed through due diligence and have been researched with full documentation received by Trident from all investment managers. Investments may include: ✪ World famous Investment Fund trading Currency derivatives returning 150% pa. for last 5 years ✪ Fixed Interest in the US paying 24%pa - Secured ✪ Investments with capital guarantees from major companies yielding 12-30% pa ✪ Offshore Investments yielding 50-100% pa, year after year Plus many more investments, 90% of which have never been offered to Australians. All investments are fully disclosed with entry levels from as little as a few thousand dollars. High Yield Investments is a must for all investors. **Revised and Updated Every Year. Price AUD$59.50 Best Seller!**

HIGH YIELD INVESTMENTS 2

Investments to make you wealthy
Following on from the success of the best selling *High Yield Investments - Get Rich ...Quickly!*, Lance Spicer has come up with over 60 more exciting investments that can help you attain financial independence. *High Yield Investments 2*, (*HYI 2*) continues on where the first book left off, presenting factual information on investments that have out performed and provided investors with fabulous returns. Here are a few examples of the type of investments you will find in *HYI 2*:
✪ Capital markets fund returning over 50%pa ✪ Company trading bank instruments with potentially high returns ✪ Technology investment fund returning 75%pa for the last 5 years ✪ Zero risk returns of 12% through a well respected European bank ✪ Capital guaranteed high yield investment bonds ✪ Currency fund with a potential return of nearly 100% pa. **Revised and Updated Every Year**
Price AUD$59.50 Best Seller!

Congratulations for a book (High Yield Investments) which provides a lot of financial signposts and sage comments on possible scams - HT, Melbourne

THE AUSTRALIAN SHARE MARKET GUIDE

Is it Possible to Earn a Good Living from Investing and Trading Shares on the Stockmarket? 
Many people do! The Australian Share Market Guide will show you how it's done by professional investors. The investment and trading criterion explained is similar to those used by the world's most successful share trader, billionaire Warren Buffett. Using fundamentals to select companies and buy and sell points, this book will take much of the risk out of share market investment.
Features: Value Investing - How to select undervalued shares or oversold shares - Cycles and economic factors explained - When to buy - When to Sell - What to Buy - Selection Criteria detailed - Warren Buffet's buying criteria detailed and explained - Options - Crash Strategies - Contacts and more. **Price AUD$49.50**

High Yield Investments and The Australian Share Market Guide are excellent books as they are very practical, thank you
- Ernst & Young, Accountants

The books you publish are brilliant! I have read them over several times so not to miss anything - GS, Victoria

INVISIBLE BANKING

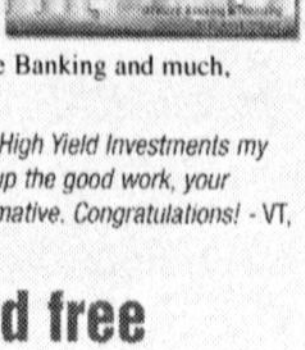

This amazing book shows you how to bank and invest offshore in total privacy
This amazing 'How To' book will provide you with the information that you always wanted to know but your accountant couldn't tell you. This entertaining book will reveal:
✪ How to keep your Banking Secret ✪ Privacy & Secrecy Tips ✪ Asset Protection Schemes ✪ How to transfer your assets and cash around the world privately ✪ Tax and Banking Strategies explained with working Examples ✪ How to establish your own offshore bank ✪ Procedures in Secret Offshore Banking and much, much more! **Price AUD$59.50 Best Seller!**

After reading Invisible Banking, The Invisible World and High Yield Investments my husband and I are very keen to invest offshore....Keep up the good work, your books are very interesting, thought provoking and informative. Congratulations! - VT, Tasmania

...for we are young and free

or are we?
Lance Spicer reveals what we all suspected, our country and our lives are becoming more controlled and our liberties are being attacked. The Australian People are becoming increasingly manipulated by the agendas of big business, banks, international interests and politicians who regard the electorate with contempt. The author discusses many of the serious issues that must be faced by all Australians: ✪ The Banking System and the hidden agendas ✪ The New World Order Organisations are exposed ✪ Loss of Privacy and what we should do about it ✪ Citizen Initiated Referenda - Take back control ✪ "Our British Constitution" proven invalid ✪ The De-Industrialisation of Australia by International interests ✪ CIA interference in our political system & spy bases pose a threat to our privacy ✪ The Dis-Arming of Australia ✪ Our Rights and Freedoms under siege *"All concerned Australians should read this book"*
Price AUD$29.50

I am writing to say how much I enjoyed your book For We are Young and Free. I am very pleased I made this purchase as it was very enlightening and should be made mandatory reading for every year 12 student before leaving school. - GT, Sydney

I have received your books, High Yield Investments and The Australian Share Market Guide a few weeks ago - I'm very impressed and thank you for the valuable information, concisely and very clearly written - RL, New Zealand

INVESTING TO WIN

Investing to Win has now been released. This book takes an aggressive, winning approach to investment that WILL achieve results from investing. This book takes a straightforward and entertaining look at all aspects of investing. It does away with all the nonsense we hear continually from the media and focuses on ways that really make money and tells you the things that don't. **The book examines**: Financial Intelligence, Share Markets, Property Investment, Superannuation, Offshore Investments, Unusual Investments, Taxation, Futures, Options, Cash Investments, Managed Funds, the Secrets of Successful Investing, Doom and Gloom, Winning Strategies, Frauds and Ripoffs & much more. This really is the complete investing guide. **Price AUD$34.50**

I have just purchased a few of your books. I have started to read the Invisible World, it's a priceless book, I couldn't put it down. I think purchasing your books is the best investment I have made. Thank you. - CL, Parramatta NSW

TRIDENT'S MINI-BOOK SERIES

Each of these A5 sized books are packed with over 50 pages of valuable information. Concise and straight to the point, these books make great gifts.

Invisible Cash
Have you ever wondered how the "professional money movers" make cash disappear in one place and reappear in another? How money launderers and criminals transfer their cash around the world? This book reveals all their tricks. A fascinating exposé on this popular subject. **AUD$24.95**

Offshore Companies & Trusts and how to use them 
These days more and more people are discovering the massive savings that can be made by having an offshore company and trust. Find out why the rich use them and why you probably should too. **Price AUD$24.95**

The Privacy Report - Strategies & Methods to beat the System! 
It seems everything we do, everywhere we go and everybody we speak to could be monitored by "someone" It's a chilling thought. No longer do we have privacy, financially or personally, but this book will empower you again. Full of strategies, methods, and simple rules to not only ensure privacy, but also to beat the system "they" have tried to impose on us. A fascinating book.
Price AUD$24.95

I was totally captivated by your books - KL, Queensland

THINGS YOU DIDN'T KNOW

Underground Knowledge 2
Like Underground Knowledge, Things You Didn't Know focuses on a wide variety of topics for the freedom lover, investor, privacy seeker, entrepreneur, Perpetual Traveller or the average person with a curious and questioning mind. For example: • Did you know there is a new 'cyber haven' where you can host your website without bureaucratic interference? This place is a relatively new nation. • Did you know that every

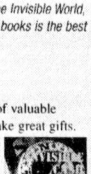

phone call you make, every fax and email you send is being monitored, right here in Australia? • Do you know where you can buy 'James Bond' type spy equipment? • Did you know there is an Australian company currently gathering all your private personal and financial details so they can sell it to the highest bidder? Do you know how it will be used? Do you know how to foil their attempts? • Ever wondered why the rich love to bank in Switzerland and why they invest in Swiss Annuities? What are Swiss Annuities? Why you should invest in them and how and with whom? • One adviser has achieved a 4,432% return for his clients this year. Would you like his name? • The same adviser has averaged 51% compound return for his clients since 1986. This man is The Guru! • There is an Australian hedge fund earning 45%pa since 1989, Do you know which one? No, it's not advertised, it's reserved for those in the know. We tell you all about it. • Another Australian fund open to everyone earning 30%pa. • Billionaire's secrets exposed • Do you want a million dollars? We show you how to get it for as little as $14 a week. • Would you like to live the life of a PT? Things You Didn't Know shows you exactly how to go about it, on any budget the right way • Second Citizenships and Passports demystified • How to hide and safeguard your assets the easy way • Plus much more! Price AUD$49.50

SCAMS & FRAUDS
Financial Crime Exposed
by Lance Spicer
Could you be ripped off in some "legitimate sounding" investment? Have you already been ripped off and don't know it? *This book may shock you - it may anger you - but it will give you the Truth.... If you can handle the Truth!* There are literally thousands of scams operating today and the problem is identifying them - This book will show you how. *The first book of its kind in the world - We name names of people still operating scams!*
Scams & Frauds features:
Bank debenture trading programs and other so-called High Yield Investment Programs • How they work, their history and why you will lose your money! • Sham Investment & Savings Clubs • Cold Callers and shonky brokers • Pyramid Schemes • MLM Shams • Ponzi Schemes -Gold Bullion and Mine scams • A List of the Biggest, Boldest and most well known scams around today that have ripped off thousands, they just don't know it... Yet! • Banks that actually steal your money • Why banking in Latvia is a HUGE mistake • Why a Bank Guarantee is No Guarantee! • Nigerian Letters • Lottery and "give away" scams • Offshore Investment scams • Fake Credit Cards • Stock market bubbles and how scamsters use them to take your money • Poor advice that leaves you...poor • Affinity fraud • Self Liquidating Loans • The truth about Pure Trusts • Internet Frauds and Scams • How to avoid being taken and what to do if you have.
Price AUD$39.50

Financial Crisis – How to avoid Financial Disaster
describes exactly how people get into great financial mess and how to get out of it, and better still how to avoid it. This enlightening and fascinating book discusses in an easy to read way how people run into financial difficulties, how to get out of them and better still how to avoid them. It is a must read for anybody concerned about money, the economy and the financial security of your family. It contains great tips and strategies to follow. 
Financial Crisis Features:
• Identifying Common Financial Problems • Money Traps • Bracing Yourself for Financial Crisis • Disaster Strikes – What To Do? • When You Can't Pay Your Bills • The Struggle for Work and Family Balance • Budgeting & Money Management • The Art of Money Control • A Strategy for Financial Recovery • Money Protection Strategies • Tips for the next 1,000 years • World v ide Financial Crisis and How to make money from it! • Prepare for The Next Stock Market Crash • People Are Telling Me To Buy Gold, Is this Wise? • The Secret to Building Wealth • Where exactly to invest and exactly what to invest in for sure fire results that work • How to make money in a falling market • Investor's Traps plus much more! Price AUD$39.50

The Author - Lance Spicer
Lance worked for many years as an accountant, senior financial executive and consultant to several major Australian and foreign corporations including Australian and foreign banks. Before 'semi-retiring', he was the financial controller of a major listed property and tourism group. In recent years, he has become a professional investor in addition to writing 25 books on various subjects such as investment, financial privacy, small business and the share market. Many of Lance's books have now attained best seller status with books having been sold in over 90 countries around the world. Lance is a regular feature writer for several leading magazines and newspapers. He has been a key speaker at several international and local seminars on issues of taxation, investment and privacy. His books have been featured on ABC Television's LateLine program and discussed on radio in the USA and in Australia. Lance's biography has recently been included in Who's Who in the World.

by Hans Jakobi

Due Diligence Made Simple
"How do I go about doing due diligence on an investment proposal?" "How do I find a good accountant, solicitor, stockbroker and real estate agent?"
Due Diligence Made Simple answers these questions and many more for you. The purpose of this book is to give you a kit bag of tools and a series of questions and techniques that you can apply in carrying out due diligence and researching something thoroughly.
Through this book, it is my intention to arm you with the necessary techniques so that you can properly understand and make an informed decision before jumping into any investment or business proposition.
It's a non-legal and non-technical book which the average investor can follow with ease. The legal eagles will be disappointed! They will no longer be able to baffle you with B.S.! **Price AUD$39.50**

How to be Rich & Happy On Your Income 2 Books Special $50
How To Be Rich & Happy On Your Income by Hans Jakobi is packed with wealth tips–both practical and esoteric. You'll discover how to:
• get beyond survival mode • manage and save money • prepare a spending plan • use credit cards wisely • minimise taxation and • increase your wealth through leverage. Easy to read and understand, this book is a down to earth collection of powerful ideas and insights, stories and experiences.

This *Action Guide* is an easy to understand companion workbook to the original *How To Be Rich & Happy On Your Income*. With the help of hands-on worksheets and carefully designed exercises, you will gain a deeper understanding of yourself and the action steps needed to propel you to the wealth and happiness you desire. **A practical, easy-to-follow money management workbook!**

12 Secrets to Wealth
Twelve Secrets To Wealth is a powerful new audio program that will reveal the secrets to making your dreams come true and has the power to change your life. This program is filled with wisdom that will make you more confident and better equipped to launch yourself into becoming the financially independent person you always wanted to be. **Price AUD$49.00**

All our books are revised and updated regularly, so rest assured the books you receive will be the latest editions available.

All the information in one discounted package including:
- **The Trident Offshore Incorporation and Investment Strategy Manual.**
- The manual is *exclusive to this special* and is valued at $95 - it is invaluable to investors
- **The Invisible World - Latest Edition** • **Invisible Banking - Latest Edition**
- **High Yield Investments 2 - Latest Edition** • **High Yield Investments - Latest Edition**
- **Offshore Companies and Trusts Book** • **Subscription to The Trident for a year**

This package contains everything you need to establish yourself offshore – all in one easy to understand package.

Value AUD$363.00, yours for only AUD$275.00 - Save AUD$88.00!
Our most popular special ever!

Visit our website at: www.tridentpress.com.au
There's plenty of free information and articles available
All our books are updated regularly so they are never out of date! All
our books are written by acclaimed Australian Author & professional
investor, Lance Spicer.
Trade and Distributorship Enquiries Welcome

I cannot tell you what a eye-opener your books are. I would like to think that I am a forward thinker with a reasonable grasp for where things are headed, but what I've read in your books has shown me up. It has been the best investment I have ever made. Knowledge is truly power, and I've been ignorant. Sincerely grateful.
- JC, Brisbane

Build your Wealth Today ... A Wealth Building Solution
We are all looking for better ways to increase our wealth but we are bombarded with differing opinions, complicated and risky schemes. It all gets too hard. However, in "Build your wealth today", the focus is on simple and logical strategies that anybody can employ to ensure they generate wealth at a rate above the "norm". A great book for people who are just starting out or don't have time for more complex solutions.
Price AUD$24.95

The Tax Haven Report Series
This range of 5 books provides the prospective offshore investor with concise information on a range of popular "tax havens". They include a synopsis, taxation and legal requirements, advantages and disadvantages, cost of establishment, regulations plus much more. Invaluable information for investors. Each book is only AUD$24.95

The Tax Haven Report 1
Panama–Belize–Caymans–Seychelles

The Tax Haven Report 2
Channel Is–Gibraltar–Isle of Man–Nevis

The Tax Haven Report 3
Liechtenstein–Luxembourg–Austria

The Tax Haven Report 4
Bahamas–Turks & Caicos–BVI–Vanuatu

The Tax Haven Report 5
Antilles–Delaware–Cook Is–Western Samoa–Barbados–Ireland

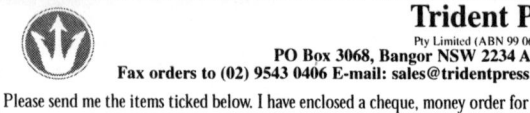

Trident Press
Pty Limited (ABN 99 065 003 045)
PO Box 3068, Bangor NSW 2234 Australia
Fax orders to (02) 9543 0406 E-mail: sales@tridentpress.com.au

Please send me the items ticked below. I have enclosed a cheque, money order for $.................. or, I have provided my credit card details below. Please allow 14 days for delivery. All prices include GST of 10% All prices in Australian Dollars.
All orders require $6.00 Postage and Handling to be added.- Only $6.00 per order

☐ Financial Crisis - How to avoid Financial Disaster $39.50+p&h
☐ Scams & Frauds - Financial Crime Exposed $39.50+p&h
☐ Things You Didn't Know - Underground Knowledge 2 $49.50+p&h
☐ Underground Knowledge - Hidden Secrets $49.50+p&h
☐ Future Wealth - The Direction of Future Fortunes $49.50+p&h
☐ The Invisible World - Financial freedom and privacy $59.50+p&h
☐ Going Out on Your Own? $19.95+p&h
☐ High Yield Investments - Get Rich.....Quickly $59.50+p&h
☐ High Yield Investments 2 - Investments to make you wealthy $59.50+p&h
☐ The Australian Share Market Guide - Latest Edition $49.50+p&h
☐ Invisible Banking $59.50+p&h
☐ ...For We are Young and Free $29.50+p&h
☐ Investing to Win $34.50+p&h
☐ Invisible Cash $24.95+p&h
☐ Offshore Companies & Trusts and how to use them $24.95+p&h
☐ The Privacy Report – Tips and Strategies $24.95+p&h
☐ Build your wealth today ... A Wealth Building Solution $24.95+p&h
☐ The Tax Haven Report 1-Panama–Belize–Caymans-Seychelles $24.95+p&h
☐ The Tax Haven Report 2-Channel Is-Gibraltar-Isle of Man-Nevis $24.95+p&h
☐ The Tax Haven Report 3-Liechtenstein-Luxembourg-Austria $24.95+p&h
☐ The Tax Haven Report 4-Bahamas-Turks & Caicos-BVI-Vanuatu $24.95+p&h
☐ The Tax Haven Report 5-Antilles-Delaware-Cook Is-Western Samoa $24.95+p&h
☐ Due Diligence Made Simple by Hans Jakobi $39.50+p&h
☐ How to be Rich and Happy On your income, Book Special by Hans Jakobi $50.00+p&h
☐ Underground Knowledge 3 - Secrets of Wealth, Privacy & Offshore Investing $49.50+p&h
☐ Complete Offshore Strategy Special $275.00+p&h

Credit Card Details ☐ VISA ☐ MASTERCARD ☐ BANKARD

Card Nº ☐☐☐☐ ☐☐☐☐ ☐☐☐☐ ☐☐☐☐

Expiry date   /

Name on card _____ Signature _____

Name _____

Address _____

State _____ Postcode _____

Great Information available on our website   **www.tridentpress.com.au**